The Art of
Resin Clay

The Art of Resin Clay

Techniques for Creating Jewelry and Decorative Objects

SHERRI HAAB,

Rachel Haab, and Michelle Haab

POTTER
CRAFT

NEW YORK

Published in the United States in 2011 by Potter Craft, an imprint of the Crown Publishing Group,
a division of Random House, Inc. New York.
www.crownpublishing.com
www.pottercraft.com

POTTER CRAFT and colophon is a registered trademark of Random House, Inc.

Library of Congress Cataloging-in-Publication Data
Haab, Sherri.
 The art of resin clay : techniques and projects for creating jewelry
and decorative objects / Sherri Haab, Rachel Haab, and Michelle Haab.
     p. cm.
 Includes index.
 ISBN-13: 978-0-8230-2723-1 (alk. paper)
 ISBN-10: 0-8230-2723-6 (alk. paper)
 1. Polymer clay craft. 2. Jewelry making. I. Haab, Rachel. II. Haab, Michelle. III. Title.
 TT297.H3185 2011
 739.27—dc22
                          2011003432

Cover design by Jenny Kraemer
Cover and interior photography by Zachary Williams
Interior design by Jenny Kraemer and Laura Palese

Printed in China

First Edition

10 9 8 7 6 5 4 3 2 1

DEDICATED TO LUKE AND DAN FOR THEIR LOVE
AND SUPPORT. AND TO BABY ADELINE,
WELCOME TO OUR CRAZY, CRAFTY FAMILY.

ACKNOWLEDGMENTS

Thanks to our friends and family who encouraged us with ideas
and support. Thanks to Zachary Williams for the great photos.
Much appreciation goes to the editors, production staff,
and designers at Potter Craft who worked so hard on this book.
And a big thank-you to the artists, working with this exciting material,
who kindly provided projects and gallery photos.

Contents

Preface

Resin clay—a craft clay that contains a plastic component such as a polymer or a resin and cures without heat—is fast becoming an exciting medium for use in jewelry making and other crafts. Until recently, one-part resin clays (also referred to as air-dry clays) were often regarded only as a children's crafts material, while many two-part versions (generically known as epoxy resin clays) were familiar only to artisans and tradespeople who use them to make large-scale sculptures, industrial repairs, taxidermy, and dolls.

Our discovery and interest in resin clay came after observing an artist who used it to make a rhinestone-studded doll dress. We were impressed that the clay didn't require heat to cure, which is always required with polymer clay. We were also amazed that the resin acted as an adhesive that held the stones in place without the need for glue. These features were enough to spark our interest in its potential for jewelry making.

As we started playing around with the various clays, each of us developed her own style of working with the material. And early on, when we brought it to jewelry workshops, creative people came up with more fabulous designs than we thought possible. More features and techniques emerged quickly, and the material proved so versatile we felt compelled to share what we learned. This enthusiasm inspired the projects in this book, which we hope will be a catalyst for you to discover new ideas.

While resin clays may appear similar to polymer clays, there are differences in physical characteristics, handling, and end results that set them apart and allow them to yield unique designs. Because they don't require heating or baking to cure, heat-sensitive materials such as plastics, sequins, and pigments can be embedded into the clay. Oversize beads that are both lightweight and strong are easy to make by covering Styrofoam spheres with a thin layer of resin clay (see the Oversize-Bead Necklace, page 112). These techniques simply aren't possible with polymer clay. A material such as Styrofoam would either melt or emit toxic fumes when heated or baked.

Both one- and two-part resin clays have adhesive properties, but the two-part clays are particularly sticky, so working with them is essentially like working with moldable glue. Not only will these clays stick effortlessly to an armature or other underlying form, but materials such as embedded rhinestones or wires generally won't need a separate adhesive to create a strong bond.

Different types and brands of clay cure at different rates, which can be used to advantage when designing and creating projects. For example, you can use a quick-curing clay to create a cuff bracelet by shaping it right on your wrist (see Copper Cuff Bracelet, page 52). Other clays take longer to set up, which allows time to finesse a sculptural design, or even to start over if necessary.

Resin clays can also be made to mimic a variety of surfaces and other materials. By adding paints, pigment powders, and other inclusions, these clays can be enhanced to achieve a variety of imitative effects, including food, bone, pottery, and many others. One brand of resin clay even offers a "concrete" version that contains aggregate similar to actual concrete, which helps give it a rough, realistic appearance.

As we worked with the clays to better understand their components and characteristics, we found a few welcome surprises that led to new techniques. With two-part resin clay, for example, we discovered that laser-printer images can be easily transferred simply by pressing the image onto the uncured clay surface while still soft. We then realized that this feature could be used to replicate painted or antique effects such as scrimshaw, porcelain, or vintage tintypes.

With their many distinctive properties, we think you'll find resin clays to be an exciting addition to your jewelry- and craft-making supplies. As you use them, you'll be discovering a new crafts medium, along with techniques you may never have thought were possible to achieve with any other clay medium.

....

Resin Clay Essentials

Resin clay is an exciting new medium for serious jewelry making. There are many brands available from suppliers who carry sculpting clays. Most resin clays can be found online, and a few brands are now in craft stores. Resin clays vary in formulation, color options, texture, strength, and curing times. We divide the clays in this book into two basic types: two-part resin clays and air-dry clays. You'll find that some of the same general information applies to each type, regardless of brand. For example, all two-part resin clays are mixed in a one-to-one ratio. And two-part clays "cure," whereas air-dry clays "dry." In this chapter, you'll learn basic guidelines for working with these clays, as well as for sculpting, adding color, and understanding curing times and strength properties.

Whenever you start using a new material, it's important to familiarize yourself with techniques first. Make small sample pieces to test curing times, and to see if the properties of a particular clay will suit your project. Experiment with tools, art supplies, and found objects that will spark your creativity. Art and craft supply stores have many of the supplies you will need to make projects with resin clay. Additional supplies for making jewelry can be found at jewelry suppliers or local bead shops. In the craft store, check the aisle where polymer clay is sold to find small cutting tools, molds, and clay sculpting tools. You'll find resources for all of the clays mentioned here, as well as tools and jewelry-making supplies, on page 141.

Types
of
Resin Clay

We've divided the resin clays used in this book into two categories to distinguish the properties unique to each group: air-dry and two-part resin clays. Both contain a plastic component (either a polymer or a resin) and cure to a strong, flexible material without the application of heat. The curing process for air-dry clay begins once it's unwrapped and exposed to the air, gradually hardening as the moisture in the clay evaporates. By contrast, two-part resin clays will cure only when the two components—clay and catalyst—are properly mixed together. This section explains the other important differences between the two types of resin clays, the various brands within each type, and their general working properties.

AIR-DRY RESIN CLAYS

There are many different brands and types of clay that are referred to as "air-dry." They're made from a wide variety of materials, from nylon fibers to flour. This book focuses on air-dry resin clays, which contain plastic components that give them strength and flexibility.

Air-dry resin clays cure when exposed to air and harden from the outside in as the moisture within them evaporates. As a result, we found that these clays are best suited for making small, delicate, and thin pieces and elements. Large or thick pieces made with air-dry clays often take much longer than the manufacturer's general estimated curing time to fully cure, so we suggest that you work over an armature or other framework when using them for those applications.

Because the curing process for air-dry resin clays doesn't involve a chemical reaction that may release fumes, they're considered safer and therefore don't have the same handling requirements as two-part resin clays (which are discussed below); they can even be used by children. The brands of air-dry clays used in this book are also acid-free and nontoxic.

It should be noted that air-dry resin clays are generally less durable than two-part clays, and don't function as adhesives as two-part clays do. Air-dry clay will stick to itself, but embedded elements must be secured with glue after the clay cures.

LUMINA

Lumina clay is made in just one color—a creamy white—that's slightly translucent. The clay is sold in an airtight package and can be found online or in select retail stores alongside other sculpting clays. It is incredibly durable and holds up well for fine work.

Lumina can be worked as is, right out of the package, or colored with the addition of oil or acrylic paints or pigments (see page 26 for more information). One of Lumina's best properties is its extreme flexibility and durability when rolled into very thin sheets. Once cured, a sheet of Lumina can be cut with craft scissors into various shapes, or even stitched with a sewing machine.

- **Feel:** Soft, smooth, moist, and pliable; fine clay particles that are easy to manipulate.
- **Finish:** Matte; especially translucent in thin layers; the surface can be altered with paint and other finishes.
- **Drying/curing time:** Dries in about 1½ hours; cures fully in 24 hours.
- **Applications:** For delicate projects that are thin and require durability and flexibility, or anything that requires a translucent, porcelain-like look.

MAKIN'S CLAY

Makin's Clay is known for its strength and a certain flexibility that makes it resistant to breaking. This brand comes in many different colors—a range of nine basic colors, plus four neon colors and a glow-in-the-dark version—which makes it easy to mix a wide range of  colors. If you need custom colors or other effects, you can add acrylic or oil paint to the clay.

- **Feel:** Slightly sticky but smoothes out as it's kneaded.
- **Finish:** Matte, opaque; paint adheres easily to cured clay. The surface can be stained, or textured to change the finish.
- **Drying/curing time:** Dries in about 1¼ hours; cures fully in 24 hours.
- **Applications:** Small jewelry pieces, sculptures, and home decor projects. For thick or sculptural pieces, it's best to form over Styrofoam or some other armature material to provide structure and to facilitate even drying.

OTHER AIR-DRY RESIN CLAYS

There are numerous other air-dry clays on the market. Many are used to make figurines or to replicate items such as realistic food. Lightweight clays such as Hearty, Cloud Clay, or Model Magic are worth mentioning because they're sold and used frequently with other resin clays. These clays may not be strong or flexible enough to be used alone for a particular design, but can be used in conjunction with other resin clays. A clay such as Hearty looks like frosting or whipped cream and is fun to use to make fake desserts with (see page 92). Because the clays are lightweight they also make good bead cores or armatures over which other types of clay can be layered.

ClayCraft by Deco is another brand of air-dry resin clay. This clay can be fashioned into any shape, especially ultra-thin and delicate pieces. It's available in six colors, and endless color-mixing possibilities make it perfect for detail work. Examples of detailed flowers that have been sculpted with this clay are hard to discern from the real thing. The brand also offers an extensive education program, with many classes designed to help prospective artists with advanced techniques.

TWO-PART RESIN CLAYS

The two-part resin clays that are featured in this book are those that cure when two components—one containing the resin portion of the clay and the other a catalyst—are mixed together. (Clays that require a catalyst in order to cure are sometimes referred to as "epoxy resin putty" or simply "resin clay.") The combination of resin and catalyst triggers a chemical reaction called polymerization, which links monomer molecules into polymer chains, resulting in a hard plastic.

Two-part resin clays offer jewelry artists and designers many advantages. In addition to their adhesive properties, the clays are particularly strong, which makes even delicate jewelry pieces and sculptures extremely durable. This strength also allows two-part resin clays to be sanded, sawed, drilled, and filed without cracking after they're cured. Many brands also boast minimal or no shrinkage after curing.

It's important to note that not all two-part resin clays have the same working characteristics and curing times. Some cure within minutes, while others take hours. It's best to test the clay you intend to use before you start a project in order to familiarize yourself with its working properties and other attributes. Experimenting with the clay will minimize frustration and prevent project failures. Unlike other craft clays, two-part resin clay is permanent, so once you push or shape it into a bezel or sculpt it over an armature, it's not going anywhere. This reliability is actually one of its best features, but it can be challenging and even problematic if the clay cures before you've finished forming it. It's important to understand what to expect from a particular brand before you begin working with it to create a new piece of jewelry or other object.

Resin Clay Flower Bracelets by Sherri Haab. Two-part resin clay, acrylic paint, and fabric.

Aves Studio offers a variety of clays, including both air-dry and two-part resin types. They offer great tutorials and comparison charts that detail the properties and advantages of the various clays. We like using Apoxie Sculpt in particular; it's different than most two-part clays because it's available in a range of colors and has a plastic putty feel to it.

Apoxie Sculpt brand of two-part resin clay looks very similar to polymer clay, but it's very strong once it cures, which makes it ideal for jewelry. It's one of the most widely used resin clays on the market and has long been used by taxidermists, sculptors, and prop and special-effects artists for various applications. The clay, which comes in several colors, can be mixed to create custom shades. One advantage of this product is that it cures very slowly, which allows the user to make adjustments and spend a great deal of time on details. Apoxie Sculpt can also be smoothed with water.

Aves also carries a product called Aves Safety Solvent that softens the clay for blending and thinning.

- **Feel:** Very smooth and easy to mix; can become sticky if it gets too warm. Feels like taffy and holds its shape as it cures.
- **Finish:** Very low-sheen, semigloss, somewhat plastic appearance; can be altered by sanding or applying other surface treatments.
- **Curing time:** Begins to cure in 2 hours; cures fully in 24 hours.
- **Applications:** Sculptures, beads, and any projects where bright color is preferred. Use when long curing time is preferred to allow for changes or adding complex details. Holds embedded elements such as rhinestones well.

The various types of KlayResin—concrete, copper, steel, and porcelain—are sold in small cylinders in which an inner core of Part A (the catalyst) is surrounded by a layer of Part B (the clay color). To use this brand, simply cut off a section of the clay with a craft knife or blade, being sure to make the cut very straight to ensure an equal amount of each part in the portion. Knead the two parts together well. You may notice the clay warming as it begins to catalyze. You can mix fillers or pigment into the clay as you combine the catalyst with the clay; however, note that you have only a small window of working time. Test the filler you intend to add with a small amount of clay to make sure it doesn't inhibit curing.

KlayResin is different from the other brands of two-part resin clay in how quickly it catalyzes: It begins to set up in only 3 to 5 minutes and fully cures within 24 hours. The speed of this process can be very beneficial in some circumstances; for example, this clay can be used to create a cuff bracelet directly on your wrist, which allows you to control the shape to achieve a perfect fit (see Copper Cuff Bracelet, page 52, for an example). A quick-setting clay is also good for workshops that require projects to be completed in a limited amount of time.

Another distinctive quality of KlayResin is its unique faux-finish formulas that look just like the real thing, making it easy to create projects out of clay instead of having to use the actual materials themselves. And although image transfer can be achieved with other two-part resin clays, we've found that this brand is usually the most successful and yields the clearest images. (Learn more about the image transfer process in the scrimshaw project on pages 40–44.)

- **Feel:** Slightly sticky at first, then smooth once kneaded. The Concrete formula contains aggregate and thus has a grittier hand.
- **Finish:** Mostly matte; can be buffed to a low sheen.
- **Curing time:** Begins to cure in 10–30 minutes; cures fully in 24 hours.
- **Applications:** Small jewelry pieces; chain links because the clay sets up fast; projects requiring imitative effects such as bone, china, concrete, and metal; particularly good for image transfers. Good for workshops where time is essential.

MAGIC-SCULPT

Magic-Sculpt clay is packaged in two separate containers, one containing the resin clay and one containing the hardener. The clay is available in white, black, brown, green, and pink; paint can be added to uncured clay to make custom colors and effects, or applied afterward to the cured surface. Pieces made with Magic-Sculpt have a slight roughness that allows paint to adhere nicely to the cured surface.

Magic-Sculpt is one of the epoxy clays that smoothes well with water. Simply dip your fingers in water and lightly smooth out any imperfections in the surface of the clay. It's a nice clay to work with because it washes off your hands easily with water.

- **Feel:** Smooth; not very sticky compared to other two-part resin clays.
- **Finish:** Matte, slightly chalky, porous, inflexible finish; similar in weight to stone or ceramic; surface can be painted or stained.
- **Curing time:** Begins to cure in 1½ hours; cures fully in 24 hours.

- **Applications:** Larger sculptural objects; thick or solid pieces that won't endure stress or bending; figures that rely on painted details.

MILLIPUT

Milliput is a well known, time-tested epoxy clay that's often used by miniaturists and model makers. It's been around since the 1960s, and a few colors were introduced in the 1980s. The clay comes in several colors—white, silver-gray, yellow-gray, terra cotta, and black—and can be mixed with paint or pigment powder if a different hue is desired. The cured clay can also be painted with acrylics.

Milliput comes in two separate cylinders of clay. One part is the resin clay and the other part is the catalyst. Pinch or slice away equal amounts of each part and mix them together well. The manufacturer suggests kneading well for about 5 minutes to make sure they're fully combined. Water can be used to smooth this clay while it's still soft. Milliput is manufactured by a U.K.-based company, but it can be purchased through many online retailers or hobby shops.

- **Feel:** Very smooth; not overly soft or sticky.
- **Finish:** Mostly matte; can be sanded, carved, or drilled after the clay is cured.
- **Curing time:** Begins to cure in 1½ hours; cures fully in about 8 hours.
- **Applications:** Small miniatures and beads; natural colors mimic organic materials such as bone or stone.

Tools
and
Supplies

There are many different tools on the market made specifically for use with sculpting and modeling clays that can also be used with resin clay. We recommend that you dedicate a set of these tools exclusively for use with resin clay, as they may become coated with cured clay over time. To clean your tools, wash them in hot water and soap, or wipe them with rubbing alcohol or other solvent to dissolve excess uncured clay. Products vary, so check to see which cleaning method is best according to the manufacturer.

The following is a list of the tools we used most frequently for the projects in this book, along with a description of each. Experiment with these and other tools you may have on hand to find out what works best for you.

BASIC TOOLS

The great thing about working with resin clay is that your tool kit can be very simple; many of the tools are just ordinary household items. Most hobby and craft stores carry clay tools, textures, and cutters that will work perfectly for resin clay projects. Look for polymer clay or sculpting tools used for ceramics for most of the basics.

OLIVE OIL: Because resin clay can be very sticky, olive oil is an essential tool for resin clay artists. Rub it onto work surfaces to make them nonstick. Dip the sharp ends of cutters into oil and brush it into molds as a release agent. Besides helping you remove the cutters and molds from the clay, oil will help you get a cleaner cut without torn edges and will protect your tools from sticky clay. Some artists use cooking spray, petroleum jelly, or Badger Balm as a release agent.

RUBBER GLOVES: Nitrile gloves are a particularly good choice for working with resin clay. They're an alternative for people who are sensitive to latex, and the nitrile is less likely to break down or react with the resin. We minimize contact with the clay, first by wearing gloves during the conditioning or mixing stage, which can be very messy. After mixing, we remove the gloves and oil our hands with olive oil to keep the clay from sticking as we form and sculpt with it. Although it's easier to manipulate clay when you can feel it with your bare hands, some people can be sensitive to plastics and may develop dermatitis. Depending on the brand of clay you're using, take care to read about safety measures and wear gloves if necessary, especially with repeated contact.

PLASTIC ROLLER: The roller we use to roll out thin sheets of clay is made of a smooth plastic, and it can be oiled lightly to prevent sticking. A smooth drinking glass or cut plastic pipe can also be used as a roller. In addition to making smooth sheets, a roller can be used to press sheets of clay onto a texture plate or surface.

WATER SPRAY BOTTLE: Keep air-dry clay hydrated and smooth. Some types of two-part resin clays can be smoothed with water.

RUBBER-TIPPED CLAY SHAPER: There are many different varieties of clay shapers, which can be found at art supply stores or from polymer and metal clay suppliers. We prefer one with a stiff rubber tip for creating small details, texturing, and helping with attachments. Shapers with rounded rubber tips are wonderful for moving clay around gently. A blunt rubber-tipped tool will also help to smooth a roughly cut edge.

NEEDLE TOOL OR TOOTHPICK: Piercing holes in clay in order to attach findings, creating stippled textures, or working in very small areas all are best done with a needle tool or round toothpick. Some needle tools feature a tapered design that allows the user to gradually enlarge the size of a hole, which reduces the chance of tearing or distorting the clay.

WOODEN SKEWER OR HEAVY WIRE: To make beads, use a wooden skewer or a heavy-gauge wire to pierce holes through the clay. Gently pierce the shaped bead with the skewer or wire, reshape the bead as needed, then twist the skewer or wire gently to remove it before the clay hardens on it permanently.

RING MANDREL: Rings can easily be made with resin clay on a mandrel, which is used as a form to shape the ring and help maintain the desired size. We recommend using a stepped or multisized mandrel set to avoid the size distortion that can occur when using a tapered mandrel. Before you begin working with resin clay, tape a strip of Teflon around the mandrel to prevent the clay from sticking to it.

PAINTBRUSHES: Brushes come in a variety of shapes and sizes that can be used for different purposes: applying pigment powder to the surface of uncured clay, painting finished pieces, and applying varnish. Acrylic types, including rounds and flats, as well as inexpensive disposable brushes all come in handy.

WET/DRY SANDPAPER: To refine the surface of cured clay to prepare it for painting, we recommend using 600-grit wet/dry sandpaper. Use sandpaper with water to avoid dust particles that result from sanding plastic. Sand or polish until the desired finish is achieved. Coarser grits can be used if more material needs to be removed. Finer sanding grits and polishing tools made for plastics are also applicable for cured resin clay.

DRILL OR PIN VISE: You can use a hand drill (such as a Fiskars hand drill) or a pin vise to drill holes in fully cured clay. We found that drilling by hand produces better results than using a high-speed electric drill. Manually operated tools will ensure the slow speed that's necessary to drill smoothly through the clay and to avoid the resin from melting on the drill bit.

WORK SURFACES

Resin clay will stick to almost any surface; once cured, it can be impossible to remove. Also, resin clays will react negatively with certain plastics used to make or coat tabletops, dissolving or permanently staining the surface. Due to the fact that plastics may react, make sure that you always cover your worktable with one of the following materials in order to protect it and your jewelry piece.

TEFLON SHEETS: The best work surface for resin clay is Teflon. Teflon sheets are nonstick and won't react with the chemistry of the clay. Projects can even be left on Teflon to cure and will simply lift off the sheet when fully dry. Teflon sheets can also be cut into small strips and taped around ring mandrels or forms to protect tools and allow rings and other pieces to slide off easily when cured. Teflon is available from rubber-stamp suppliers and is also sold as a baking or ironing accessory.

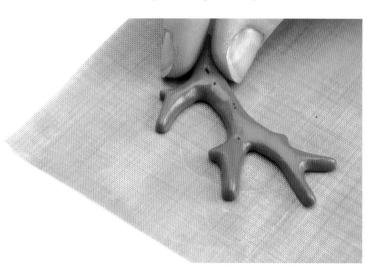

WAXED PAPER: Waxed paper should only be used as a work surface with resin clay while the clay is being actively molded or worked. Note that if the clay is pressed onto waxed paper, it will stick to it as it cures. If you would like to leave pieces on waxed paper to dry, be sure to prepare the paper by first applying a thin coat of olive oil. If waxed paper gets stuck to a cured piece, use your fingernails to pull away as much of the paper as you can, then sand the piece under water using 600-grit wet/dry sandpaper to remove any remaining paper residue.

CUTTING TOOLS

Cutting tools include knives, blades, and shaped cutters. Polymer clay suppliers as well as kitchen stores offer a variety of cutting tools appropriate for use with resin clay. Just keep these separate from those you use for food.

CRAFT KNIFE: Use it to cut shapes out of sheets of clay, to score lines, and to cut away excess clay. A craft knife can also be used to carve and scrape cured clay to achieve an antiqued or distressed look (see the Scrimshaw Pendant on page 40).

MAT-CUTTER BLADE: A mat-cutter blade can be used to create a straight cut in uncured clay, and to chop up cured thin sheets of clay into bits that can be embedded to add texture (see the realistic mini food on pages 92–100). These blades are sold at art stores where framing supplies are sold.

POLYMER CLAY BLADES: Extra long, flexible blades are also useful for cutting straight edges or even curves.

SHAPED CUTTERS: Tiny cookie cutters and cutters made for polymer clay provide perfect shapes every time. Manufactured by Kemper Tools, Klay Kutters are available in a variety of shapes. Make sure to dip the sharp end of the cutter in olive oil to yield a clean cut and to keep the cutter from sticking to the clay.

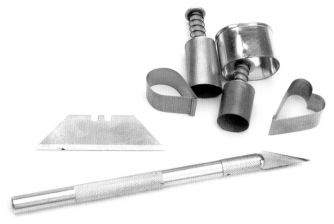

TEXTURING TOOLS

There are a variety of texture plates, press molds, and rubbing plates that can be found in craft supply shops and online. You can also use rubber stamps and leather embossing tools to create unique motifs in your jewelry. Be sure to oil these to prevent sticking.

Objects that can be used to create textures in clay can be found everywhere! Many of the projects in this book have been textured using antique buttons, found objects—even the patterns found on old silverware (see the Hollow Pendant, page 124). Organic materials such as leaves and branches can also be used, as well as fabric, lace, and even decorative picture frames.

Plastic, metal, glass, and organic materials used to texture clay will need to be brushed with olive oil as a release agent. Coat the surface of the item with olive oil by applying it with a cotton ball or brush.

TOOLS FOR REFINING AND FINISHING

In addition to sanding and buffing by hand, you can also use a bench lathe to sand and polish cured resin clay. Note that bench grinders or lathes sold at hardware stores usually run at speeds that are too high for polishing resin. Instead, use various wheels on a jeweler's lathe featuring a low rpm of 500–1500, which can accommodate plastic. Jeweler's lathes can be found wherever lapidary or jewelry tools are sold.

Working
with
Resin Clay

This section presents guidelines for working with both air-dry and two-part types of resin clay. Since the clays may be unfamiliar to you, it's helpful to have a few working tips and safety guidelines to help you along the way.

Before you begin, it's important to note mixing different types of clays together may result in failure. Even for clays of the same type, the chemical composition of one brand may not be compatible with another, which could inhibit the curing process and thus compromise the integrity of your finished piece. The only exception to this would be clays of similar formulations that are offered by the same manufacturer or company. For example, Hearty Clay can be mixed with Lumina to make a lovely hybrid-type clay as specified by the manufacturer. Make sure it's sound and safe to mix clays to avoid problems. Always follow the advice of the manufacturing companies, who have tested their products extensively. You can often find more safety information (and project ideas) on their websites than you'll find on the package or wrapper.

SAFETY GUIDELINES

The air-dry resin clays featured in this book—Lumina and Makin's—carry the AP (Approved Product) nontoxic seal of the Art & Creative Materials Institute, Inc. (ACMI). According to the ACMI website, AP-rated products have been certified "to contain no materials in sufficient quantities to be toxic or injurious to humans, including children, or to cause acute or chronic health problems," which makes them safe for children ages twelve and older to use.

When working with two-part resin clays, wearing gloves made of nitrile is a good practice, especially during mixing or heavy use to avoid dermatitis or other allergic reactions. It's also wise to wear gloves when mixing in paint, even for air-dry clays that are safe. Since each brand of clay is different, be sure to follow the manufacturer's guidelines for safety information, including whether and when to wear gloves or other protective gear.

We've found that it isn't necessary to wear a dust mask while mixing resin clay. However, when working with any type of pigment powder or metallic powder, a dust mask must be worn to prevent inhalation of particles. Remember also to wear a dust mask when dry-sanding any type of cured clay, both air-dry and two-part.

Clays should *never* be ingested or used for items that will come into contact with food. Some clays may cause eye or mucous membrane irritation if not used properly. Make sure to follow the manufacturer's age recommendations for nontoxic clays, and keep certain clays out of reach of children.

GETTING READY

When working with resin clay, *never* wear jewelry (such as rings) that might come into contact with the clay. Resin clay is designed to stick to everything, so there's a chance that it can stick to your ring and never come off! Clean hands, gloves, or a little oil helps to keep the clay from collecting on your skin.

Some varieties of resin clay can set up very quickly, so it's best to think about your piece and prepare everything you need before you even begin. First, start by making a sketch of your design, or at least have a clear idea of what you want to create. Otherwise, you may end up with a hardened, unfinished solid lump while you attempt to design on the fly. Second, make sure you have all of your tools and supplies at hand so you can work quickly.

Another factor to bear in mind when you begin a project is the temperature of your work environment, which can affect how quickly the clay cures. Resin clays, both air-dry and two-part, will harden more quickly in a warm room than they will in a cold one. If you need to extend your clay's working time, work in a cooler room. Water will help keep water-soluble clays hydrated in hot, dry environments.

AIR-DRY RESIN CLAYS

Begin working with your air-dry resin clay by cutting or pinching off part of a block and conditioning by kneading it in your hands for about 30 seconds. Once it's kneaded, the clay can be combined with pigments, acrylic paints, or oil paints to create custom colors or special effects (see page 26). Whenever you're working with any brand of air-dry resin clay, always make sure to store the portion of the package you aren't using in an airtight container.

Because water is a component of air-dry resin clays, it can be used to prolong their working time. As the clay is exposed to air while you're working with it, it may begin to dry out before you're finished. If that happens, you can knead in a little water to keep it moist, dampen it by spritzing it with water from a spray bottle, or cover it with a damp cloth to keep it from hardening. Water can also be brushed on the clay to create a tacky surface or mixed with a bit of clay until the clay is sticky or tacky enough to make a self-adhesive "glue." The sticky surface will then allow pieces to stick or to be added on.

TWO-PART RESIN CLAYS

The resin and catalyst portions of all the two-part resin clays in this book are mixed together in one-to-one ratios—that is, in equal parts—and must be mixed thoroughly in order to cure properly. A good way to check that you've fully mixed the two components together is by making sure the color of the mixture is completely uniform. There should be no "marbling" or visible streaks after the two parts have been combined. If you see any swirls of color, continue mixing until the clay is one uniform color throughout. You may feel the clay warm as you mix its two components and the mixture begins to catalyze.

By wearing gloves while you're mixing your two-part clay, your hands will be cleaner when the clay is ready to be sculpted. Adding oil to your hands after removing the gloves will minimize the sticking.

1. Wearing gloves, make two balls of clay, one of resin and one of catalyst. Make sure the balls are the same size. If you're working with a two-part clay that's sold with both parts rolled together in a cylinder shape with the catalyst running down the center, simply slice a section from the cylinder of clay and proceed to the next step.

2. Press the balls of clay together and begin mixing them. Knead the clay by repeatedly folding it in half, then in half again. If your gloves become too sticky and coated with clay during this process, knead the clay by rolling it between your palms into a thick rope. This motion will pick up most of the excess clay from your gloves. Fold the rope in half lengthwise and roll another rope. Continue until fully mixed.

3. Knead until the clay is fully mixed. If the clay you're working with cures quickly, you must begin shaping it right away before it catalyzes. If your clay is slow setting, you can let it sit for a few minutes before you begin your project.

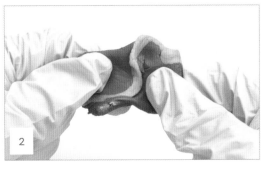

CURING GUIDELINES

We created the timing guidelines below to help you to choose the right clay for your project. Before choosing a type or brand of resin clay, you should take into account how much time you'll need to sculpt your design and embed any objects you're planning to incorporate.

We performed the tests for this chart under regular home conditions—at an average temperature of 70°F (21°C) with normal airflow. We didn't add any moisture to the clay as we worked with it, and we handled each clay sample minimally.

Please keep in mind that curing times can vary, depending on a few factors:

- **Temperature:** In a warmer environment, resin clay will cure more quickly. A cold room will extend the clay's working time.
- **Handling:** If clay is handled extensively, it can collect warmth from the artist's hands and cure more quickly. Less clay-to-hand contact and sculpting minimally and gently will allow a piece to cure more slowly.
- **Size:** Larger pieces cure more slowly because they have more surface area, while small pieces will cure faster.
- **Moisture:** Adding water to air-dry clays can extend their working time. Just spritz a little bit of water onto the clay's surface or knead it in to keep it moist and slow drying time.

STRENGTH CHARTS

Compared with other types of crafts clay, resin clays are some of the strongest and most durable. Depending on the project you're creating, flexibility may be a preferred feature; in others, strength may be the most important.

To help you choose the best clay for your piece, we recorded the results of two tests we performed on fully cured, doughnut-shape rings of equal size and width—a pressure test using a vise, and a snap test using pliers—in the tables below.

STRENGTH COMPARISON

Air-Dry Clays		
	Strength	Flexibility
Lumina	Moderately weak	Very high
Makin's	Weak	Moderately high

Two-Part Clays		
	Strength	Flexibility
Aves Apoxie Sculpt	Medium high	Medium low
KlayResin	High	Moderately low
Magic-Sculpt	Very high (strongest)	Very low
Milliput	Very high	Low

CURING TIME COMPARISON

Air-Dry Clays					
	Conditioning time	Initial moisture loss	Stiff but still workable	No longer workable	Fully cured
Lumina	30 seconds	10 minutes	1 hour	1½ hours	24 hours
Makin's	30 seconds	7 minutes	50 minutes	1¼ hours	24 hours

Two-Part Clays				
	Mixing time	Stiff but still workable	No longer workable	Fully cured
Aves Apoxie Sculpt	2 minutes	1 hour	2 hours	24 hours
KlayResin	1 minute	5 minutes	8 minutes	24 hours
Magic-Sculpt	2 minutes	40 minutes	1½ hours	24 hours
Milliput	3 minutes	1½ hours	1½ hours	8 hours

CLEANING UP

Resin clay is always easier to remove from your hands and surfaces while it's still soft. In most cases you can quickly wipe away unhardened clay from surfaces with soap and water or wet wipes, but there are some other products you should be aware of that will take care of more challenging messes.

SOAP AND WATER: Basic hand soap and water are usually enough to clean sticky hands or to quickly wipe away uncured clay from a surface. Use warm water and roll away the clay from your hands as you wash them.

WET WIPES: It's helpful to keep a box of wet wipes or baby wipes with you while you're working with the clay to wipe residue off your fingers in between colors or for quick cleanups. The best wipes to use with resin clay are sanitizing wipes made for babies or toddlers. These products contain alcohol, which acts as a solvent for removing clay. We prefer brands that don't leave loose fibers behind, and suggest that you purchase small travel-size packages to find one that works well.

FAST ORANGE: Fast Orange is a soap often used by auto mechanics to clean grease and tough grime off their hands. This product, which can be found in variety stores or auto supply shops, is also great for removing resin clay from hands when plain soap and water just aren't enough. Fast Orange contains pumice, which helps scrub away caked-on resin clay from your hands. Rub the product into your hands without any water to dissolve the clay, then use warm water to wash away the soap and clay residue.

RUBBING ALCOHOL: Rubbing alcohol right out of the bottle can also be used as a solvent for cleaning up resin clay. Before the clay cures, dip a cotton ball or swab in alcohol to clean tools and surfaces and to wipe away clay residue from bezels, findings, and embedded objects.

SHELF LIFE AND STORAGE

Air-dry resin clays need to be tightly wrapped in plastic to retain moisture after they're opened. A vacuum-type plastic bag sealer meant for preserving food is ideal for clay storage. We use the sealer to ensure that these clays won't dry out between uses, especially when the clay is kept for an extended period. When putting away unused clay, especially air-dry clay, make sure that it's stored in an airtight container. Air-dry clays should be wrapped tightly in plastic wrap, then stored in a ziplock or vacuum-sealed plastic bag.

The shelf life of each brand of two-part resin clay varies. In general, most will last longer if kept in tightly sealed containers in a cool place. Some brands like Apoxie Sculpt recommend freezing or refrigeration to extend the life of the clay. Based on our experience, two-part resin clays remain viable for two to three years, so it's best to buy smaller amounts of fresh clay rather than trying to store it. Check the manufacturers' websites for each brand for documentation on shelf life. For example, Apoxie Sculpt reports a shelf life of three years, while Magic-Sculpt's newest formula claims to be viable indefinitely if stored in a cool place in an airtight container.

Playing
with
Color

One of the most enjoyable ways to play with resin clay is to mix colors and create new shades. Many of the clay brands featured in this book are made in different colors that can be mixed to create fantastic hues. Paints and dry pigments can also be added to both air-dry and two-part resin clays to achieve brilliant color and pearlescent or metallic effects.

MIXING CLAYS FOR COLOR

When working with air-dry resin clays, colored clays can simply be mixed together to achieve new hues, while white or neutral clays can be tinted with either liquid paints (oil or acrylic) or pigment powders. Simply knead the paint or powder into the clay until the desired shade is achieved.

In contrast, when mixing colors into two-part resin clays, the clay and catalyst parts may be packaged in separate containers. In this case, you must pre-mix the colors contained in the clay part before adding the catalyst part. This will give you time to achieve and mix a desired color before adding the catalyst. After mixing the color you can then add the appropriate amount of catalyst to the newly mixed batch of colored resin. When color mixing two-part resin clays, always be sure to mix colors from the same brand.

With two-part resin clays that are packaged in a tube with the catalyst rolled into the center, you won't be able to separate

them to mix color into the resin part only. With this type of clay, mix the color into the clay after you have begun kneading the clay. Then continue mixing. You will want to work fast as these clays cure quickly. Remember that mixing color into the clay is not your only option; color may be added to the surface in the form of paint or pigment powders.

1. Mix together different colors of just the clay part of your two-part resin clay until you achieve the color you desire.
2. Add an equal amount of the catalyst to your color mixture and mix until completely blended. Pigment powders can be applied to the surface of the clay while the clay is still tacky and not fully cured. If you want to add painted details, paint can be applied to the surface after the clay is mixed and cured.

COLORING WITH POWDERED PIGMENTS AND OTHER POWDERS

Dry powders or powdered pigments can be mixed into resin clay or brushed on the surface of uncured clay to create many different colors and effects. When working with these loose, powdered materials, be sure to always wear a dust mask to protect your lungs from inhaling particles, and check the manufacturer's warnings and instructions to see whether gloves are also required.

POWDERED PIGMENTS

A powdered pigment is a concentrated form of color that can be mixed with water or other liquid medium to create ink, paints, and dyes. When combining powdered pigments with resin clay, we mainly use them directly in their powder form. There are many different brands of powdered pigments on the market, in every color of the rainbow. Some are made from organic materials such as plants and minerals, while others are made from synthetic substances.

Pearl Ex pigments contain crushed mica, which imparts an iridescent finish. Pearl Ex pigments can also be combined with liquid pigments or colorants and mixed into clay or brushed onto its surface to add a bit of pearlescent shine. If you choose to color your clay with powdered pigments, keep in mind that they usually yield light, somewhat pastel colors that aren't highly saturated.

Cured resin clay that has had pigment powder mixed into it (right) and applied to its surface (left).

OTHER POWDERED MEDIUMS

In addition to powdered pigments, other powdered products can be either mixed into or applied to the surface of uncured resin clay. As a rule of thumb, the color will be stronger and more concentrated if the powder is applied directly to the surface of the tacky clay. With air-dry clay, color can be mixed in to tint or alter the color of the clay. Two-part clays are more successful if the powder is applied only to the surface.

DRY TEMPERA POWDERS: This type of pigment is usually mixed with water to create tempera paint. Mix dry tempera powder with clay or apply to the surface to achieve a pastel or muted color.

METALLIC POWDERS: Metallic powders are made by grinding actual metals into very fine powders. They come in many different varieties; gold, silver, copper, bronze, and aluminum are the most common. They're applied to the surface of uncured clay, rather than mixed into it, to achieve a faux metal effect. Be sure to wear a dust mask when using metallic powders, as the small airborne particles can be harmful if inhaled. Once the clay has cured, the powdered surface can be protected with a coat of water-based varnish. (For more details on working with metallic powders, see the Copper Cuff Bracelet on page 52.)

EYE SHADOWS: Our clever workshop students who routinely use old cosmetics in their work have pointed out that eye shadows you're already likely to have around the house or can easily find in a nearby store can be a fun source of beautiful, iridescent color. Use a toothpick to crush up some eye shadow, scoop it onto your clay, then knead to distribute it throughout the mixture. Don't use eye shadow on yourself once you've used it with your crafting tools and materials.

MIXING POWDERED PIGMENT INTO CLAY

This method shows how to incorporate pigment powders into the clay. You could also mix glitter, sand, or other fillers to change the texture of the clay.

1. Shape a small amount of clay into a flat disk. Lightly tap some powdered pigment into the center of the disk. You can also use a toothpick to scoop up a small amount of pigment and place it on the clay. Don't use excessive amounts of powder, as it can dry out the clay and make it crumble.
2. Fold the clay in on itself and knead it well to distribute the powder evenly throughout.
3. The mixed clay with the powdered pigment fully incorporated.

APPLYING POWDERED PIGMENT TO UNCURED CLAY

Powdered pigments can also be applied to the surface of resin clay. The powder adheres well to the uncured clay and won't rub off easily. It's fun to roll a bead in Pearl Ex pigments to give it a pearlescent look. A raised or embossed texture, even one as light and subtle as a fingerprint, can be highlighted by lightly brushing it with the powder.

You can control the coverage of the pigment to some extent by timing its application to the curing of the clay. Powder will adhere better to sticky clay and produce a more saturated color. If you want to create a less saturated color or blend colors, it's easier to apply the pigments to a surface that has cured longer and is less tacky.

1. After you've finished sculpting or molding your design, use your finger or a paintbrush (according to the manufacturer's directions) to dust the surface of the uncured clay with powder.
2. Dust away any excess powder and let the piece cure fully.

COLORING WITH PAINTS AND LIQUID PIGMENTS

A variety of different paints and liquid mediums—acrylics, oils, and alcohol inks—can be used to accent and enhance resin clay projects. Compared with powdered mediums, paints and liquid pigments yield stronger, more vibrant colors when mixed with resin clay. You can also paint designs on cured clay, or use inks to enhance textures.

ACRYLIC PAINTS: Acrylics are a widely available and somewhat inexpensive way to color resin clay. Keep in mind that adding acrylic paint to clay can make it stickier, which won't hinder the curing process but may make it more challenging to work with. Acrylics are also ideal for changing the surface color of cured clay. Try rubbing a bit of brown or black acrylic paint onto the surface of your piece with a soft cloth to create an antique effect (see Faux Scrimshaw Pendant on page 40).

OIL PAINTS: Oil paint is very concentrated, so you'll get a strong, slightly translucent color by using just a small amount. Do not apply oil paint to the surface of cured resin clay—it won't adhere.

ALCOHOL INKS: Alcohol inks, which are commonly used for rubber stamping and other paper crafts, can also be used as colorants for resin clay.

Cured resin clay that had liquid pigment mixed into it (left) and applied to the surface of the clay after it had cured (right).

MIXING PAINT OR LIQUID PIGMENT INTO CLAY

Oil and acrylic paints, as well as inks, are great for mixing custom colors of resin clay. Only a small amount of paint is needed to yield strong color, especially when oil paint is used.

1. Flatten the soft clay into a disk. Put some paint or ink onto a sheet of waxed paper, then use a toothpick to scoop up a small amount and dab it into the center of the disk.
2. Fold the clay in on itself and knead it well to distribute the color evenly throughout. If you want to keep the color from staining you can wear gloves as you mix.

Use a brush to apply acrylic paint to the cured surface of a resin clay piece.

APPLYING PAINT OR LIQUID PIGMENT TO CURED CLAY

Acrylic paints and liquid pigments can also be applied to a fully cured project, either to completely change its surface color or to create unique designs and patterns.

Rub inks, paints, and stains into textured clay in order to create an antique finish. Use a soft cloth to rub the stain or paint into the piece and then use a damp cloth to wipe away excess pigment, leaving the recessed areas of the surface dark with pigment.

When the paint, ink, or stain has dried, you can protect the surface with a coat of water-based varnish.

MEDIUMS AND MATERIALS FOR UNIQUE SURFACE EFFECTS

Resin clay can be made to look like almost anything when you alter its texture, color, or finish. Some of these treatments work best while the clay is still soft, while others are done to cured clay.

GOLD LEAF: Gold leaf is gold that is beaten into tissue-thin sheets that can be applied to resin clay (or other materials, too) to create a metallic surface. You can use an entire sheet of leaf or tear one into small pieces. Lay a piece of leaf onto uncured clay and use a soft paintbrush to press it into the surface. A water-based varnish can be applied to protect the leaf after the clay has cured.

GLITTER, SAND, AND OTHER TEXTURAL MATERIALS: Roll still-soft clay in textural materials to completely change its surface. We have found that glitter isn't very noticeable when mixed into resin clay, so we recommend brushing or otherwise applying it to the uncured surface. Use fine glitter for surface color and shine, or chunky glass glitter for a sparkly texture. Use organic materials such as sand and crushed gravel for a natural- or faux-stone look. After you coat your piece in the material, use your fingertip to lightly press it into the clay to ensure that it will be embedded, then brush away any excess.

STAINS: Antiquing gels or acrylic stains, which are sold in craft stores that carry acrylic paints, can be applied over dried acrylic paint to create an aged look.

COLORED PENCILS: Colored pencils are great for creating multicolored designs—lettering or your own images—on cured resin clay. Use well-sharpened pencils for bold, strong lines, and dull ones for a softer look perfect for layering. Seal your finished design with a thin coat of water-based varnish.

IMAGE TRANSFERS: Toner-based images can be easily transferred directly to the surface of uncured resin clay without any additional solution. Use a laser printer or copier to print your color or black-and-white images—old posters, text, floral designs, or even family photos—on slick photo paper, then follow the directions on pages 42–43.

ACRYLIC MEDIUMS: There are many different products used to change the consistency and appearance of acrylic paints that can also be added to resin clay. The mini-food project on page 92 takes advantage of several acrylic mediums to replicate thick textures, glossy effects, and more.

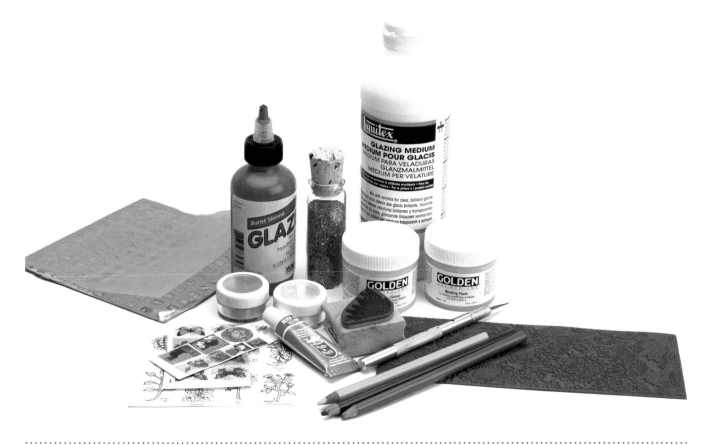

Essential Techniques

Resin clay is a new medium to most crafters, so it may be a bit tricky for beginners. To make your work easier, here are some helpful sculpting guidelines that are exclusive to working with resin clay. The basic tools discussed on pages 18–21 will help you achieve a perfectly formed piece.

WORKING IN STAGES

Being able to work on a piece in stages is one of the great benefits of using resin clay. Because it sticks to itself wonderfully and doesn't need to be baked (and thus can't be burned when adding new clay), you can start a piece, let it cure, and then add more clay to the project later. This can be beneficial in many circumstances. For instance, if you create a delicate piece and let it dry, you can go back and attach additional clay details without compressing the original form. Also, if a finding or detail breaks off, it can be easily repaired by simply adding new clay. The only disadvantage to this technique is that if a custom color has been mixed for the original piece, it can be difficult to try to recreate that color with a new batch of clay.

COOLING DOWN

When resin clay gets too hot, either from a hot room or warm hands, it can become too sticky, soft, and difficult to work with. If you take a short break and let a "hot" piece cool down for 5 to 10 minutes, the clay will become more stable and stiff, and thus much easier to work with. We used this technique as we made the Coral Branch Pendant on page 48, allowing the clay to rest periodically between forming branches, which kept the clay from stretching and sagging.

Note that some resin clays, such as KlayResin, set up too quickly to benefit from a cooling-down period.

SMOOTHING AND BLENDING

Wearing gloves while sculpting can help maintain a smooth surface by preventing fingerprints from covering your piece.

With some resin clays, you can also use water to smooth away fingerprints or to blend seams together. When adding a new attachment to an uncured piece, use a fingertip moistened with water to smooth the two pieces together, and the seam will disappear.

Some two-part resin clays, such as Aves Apoxie Sculpt, feature a corresponding solvent that can be used for smoothing and blending.

USING ARMATURES

Armatures give artists a form on which to sculpt, and they can provide structure, stability, and filler, especially for larger resin clay pieces. Because resin clays don't require heat for curing, plastics and foams can be used as armatures without any hazard. Use wire, balls of aluminum foil, pieces of foam, or even cardboard as a base for your projects. Check out the Graffiti Bracelet on page 84 and the Oversize-Bead Necklace on page 112 for more information about working with armatures.

PROPPING PIECES

Rolled-up aluminum foil, paper, or small objects can be used to prop up an element as a piece cures to achieve a specific shape. For example, to create a clay leaf with a realistic curve, lay it over a well-oiled roll of aluminum

foil to create and maintain a natural arc as it dries. Make sure that any material you use as a prop is brushed with a little olive oil so it won't stick to the clay.

EMBEDDING OBJECTS

Resin clay sticks to anything! Small objects can be embedded into the clay without any extra glue, wires, or bezels to hold them in. Simply take the piece and press it into the clay. For a little extra security, press clay around the piece to ensure that it stays in place. You can embed almost anything into resin clay: beads, sequins, buttons, marbles, game pieces, electronic parts, wires, coins, metal charms, chain, found objects, jewels, toys, and more!

TEXTURING

Any soft clay surface can be embellished with texturing tools. (Read more about different types of texturing tools on page 21.) To accentuate a textured clay surface once it has cured, rub it with paint or ink and then wipe away the excess.

CARVING

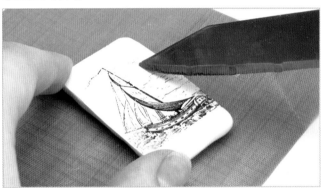

Use a craft knife to scratch irregular lines, crosshatched designs, or other patterns to add character to already cured surfaces. You can also cut into the surface of the clay at a slight angle to slice out small chunks and create a worn, antique look. Aging the surface with paint or stain will make the cracks and scratches stand out more.

Finishing

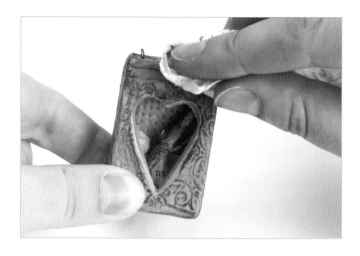

Some of your resin clay projects will require a little extra work after they've cured, whether to achieve a glossy shine, to protect the surface, or to smooth rough edges.

SANDING

When sanding resin clay, always wear a dust mask and use wet/dry sandpaper with water. In addition to preventing the plastic from re-depositing itself into the piece, the water helps minimize airborne dust. Start with coarse grits such as 320 or 400, moving progressively higher to 600, 800, and 1000 if more refinement is required. Follow with buffing for more shine.

BUFFING

A soft sheen can be achieved by simply by rubbing a fully cured resin clay piece on your jeans or with a cloth. For a glasslike shine, buff your cured piece on a muslin wheel set at low speed (see the Coral Branch Pendant on page 48).

APPLYING WATER-BASED VARNISH

Water-based varnish is used in many of the projects in this book to protect painted surfaces or to seal surface treatments. Unlike other types of varnishes or sealers, which contain plastic elements that may cause the surface of the clay to discolor or become sticky, a water-based varnish won't react with resin clay. Use a soft, medium-sized paintbrush to cover your piece with a light coat of varnish, then let it dry completely. Don't forget to wash the brush with warm water and soap after you're done.

Jewelry-Making Basics

A few basic jewelry-making tools and skills are important to have. With the right tools, such as good pliers and wire cutters, you can assemble finished jewelry designs using jewelry findings. Findings are the components you'll need to assemble jewelry with. The list includes items such as wire, head pins, clasps, and jump rings, just to name a few. It's helpful to master the techniques associated with each finding. With a little practice, skills such as wire wrapping, forming loops, and closing jump rings will serve you well.

ESSENTIAL TOOLS

Pliers and wire cutters are essential hand tools for jewelry making and are used to form wire loops, to attach jump rings, and for gripping and crimping. They're made in a variety of jaw configurations, each of which facilitates a specific set of techniques. To achieve professional-quality results, you'll need a few basic types of jeweler's pliers, which don't have teeth because they're designed to bend and move metal wire without marring its surface.

ROUND-NOSE PLIERS: These pliers are used to form loops with wire; the tips of the pliers are graduated for making loops of various sizes.

CHAIN-NOSE PLIERS: Also known as flat-nose pliers, these are good, all-purpose pliers for a variety of jewelry-making techniques. They're used to open and close jump rings and to grip wire and hold it in place as you twist, wrap, or make connections with it.

NEEDLE-NOSE PLIERS: You may already own these common household pliers, which are similar to chain-nose pliers except that they have teeth that grip. We use needle-nose pliers to pull cord or wire through a stubborn bead. You can find them at any hardware store.

WIRE CUTTERS: A pair of good-quality wire cutters will cut wire neatly, especially when cutting close to a wire wrap or clipping finished wire ends. Reserve your good wire cutters for fine-gauge wires. Use inexpensive, heavy-duty cutters from the hardware store for heavy-gauge wire that would dull or even ruin your good wire cutter.

WORKING WITH FINDINGS

Findings are the parts that are used to assemble jewelry, such as clasps, pin backs, and jump rings. They come in countless sizes, metals, and finishes. Visit your local jewelry supply shop or search online stores to select the perfect pieces to complement your resin clay jewelry designs. Resin clay is unique in that many findings can be embedded directly into clay beads, brooches, and other elements before they cure instead of being fabricated traditionally.

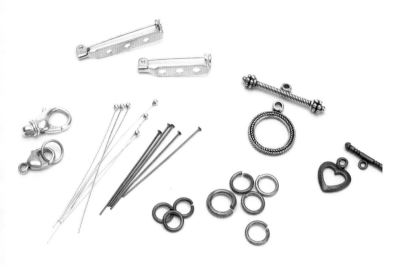

and-toggle closures are also popular because they're easy to link and give a stylish, funky look to pieces. There are many other types of clasps to choose from, including hook-and-eye and magnet-closure clasps.

JUMP RINGS

Jump rings are small metal rings that are used to link jewelry components together. They're available in base metals or in gold or silver. For a stronger jump ring, look for a heavier-gauge wire.

TO OPEN JUMP RINGS: *Always* twist the ends out sideways with pliers; *Don't* pull them apart. Opening the jump rings the wrong way adds stress to the metal. Close them the same way you opened them, bringing the ends back together by moving them sideways until they touch in the middle.

HEAD PINS

These are wires with a ball or flat pad on one end; they're used to add bead dangles to projects. Thread a bead or beads onto a head pin, then use round-nose pliers to form a loop to attach the dangle to your project. Use wire clippers to cut off the excess wire. Uncured resin clay can also be threaded onto a head pin, allowed to cure, and then attached as a dangle.

EYE PINS

Eye pins are similar to head pins except that they have a loop instead of a pad or ball at one end. The loop allows you to link pieces or add bead dangles.

PIN BACKS

Pins and brooches can be made by adding pin backs to those projects. These findings are available in silver or gold and come in varying lengths. They can be attached either by embedding them into uncured clay or by gluing them to a cured piece.

CLASPS

There are so many jewelry clasps available that it can be challenging to choose one that fits the style and size of your design. The lobster clasp is particularly popular because it's so easy to use: Just make a wire loop on one end of your necklace or bracelet, then attach the lobster clasp to the other end. Loop-

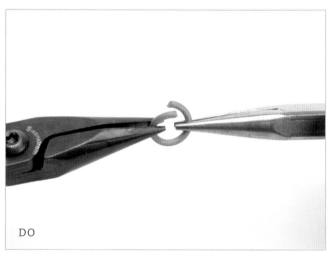

DO

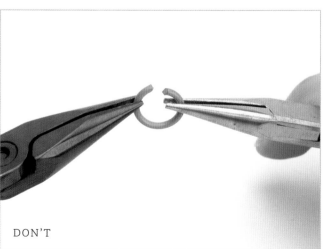

DON'T

WIRE-WRAPPING TECHNIQUES

One fundamental jewelry-making skill you'll find helpful is the ability to work with wire. Wire is used to make attachments and to create basic jewelry designs. With the right tools, such as pliers and wire cutters, it's easy to make wrapped loops and bead dangles and attach clasps. Wire is available in a variety of metals and finishes as well as gauges. Several projects in this book incorporate wire into their design. Practice your wireworking technique with inexpensive craft wire, and it will quickly become an invaluable part of your jewelry work.

MAKING A WRAPPED-WIRE LOOP

Wrapped wire is functional as well as decorative. It can be used to secure wire ends either at the base of a loop or along a section of wire to cover it. This technique can be used at the top of a head pin to create a bead dangle or to create a loop to embed into clay.

1. Make a 90-degree bend in the wire.
2. Form a loop with round-nose pliers.
3. Hold the loop with chain-nose pliers. Wrap the wire around the base of the loop a few times to secure. To connect segments of wrapped loops together, simply add a finished wrapped loop to an open loop before wrapping it.
4. Clip off the excess wire with wire cutters.
5. Tuck the end of the wire in with chain-nose pliers.

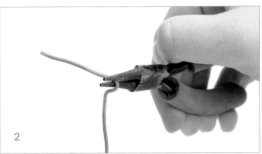

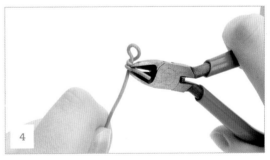

....

Imitative Techniques

Plastics have long been used to imitate other materials. In fact early plastic formulations were produced chiefly for this purpose. The demand for substitutes for scarce or expensive materials drove innovation in plastic technology. Plastics can be preferable to real materials for many reasons. It might be used to replace rare or costly substances such as gemstones, ivory, or wood. And a strong plastic may be more durable than the original object it is meant to represent. The manufacturing of a plastic may also require less labor and manipulation than forming an item from the original material. For example, a faux wood case or box could be created by pouring resin into a mold. To make the same box out of wood would require the wood to be cut, assembled, sanded, and varnished. So it is no surprise that we see plastics and composite materials all around that take advantage of the fact that materials can be imitated for practical reasons.

There are many ways to manipulate resin clays to mimic a range of natural materials, but to achieve a realistic effect, the piece must appeal to the senses. The plastic should look and feel like the real thing. Color and light reflected from a piece appeal to us visually, whereas the texture and shape appeal to touch.

Faux Scrimshaw

Genuine scrimshaw is made from carved and hand-inked whale-bone—obviously, a scarce resource. Creating beautiful faux scrimshaw with resin clay is simple: Transfer a black-and-white image to white resin clay, distress the cured piece, and then stain it with acrylic paint. The ability to transfer images is one of the many wonderful attributes of two-part resin clays. The toner from a laser-printed image bonds well with it, leaving a crisp, durable image.

KlayResin sets up very quickly for a fast and easy image transfer. The white clay was used to make the piece looks like real bone. However, the technique featured in this project can be used to transfer images to any brand or type of two-part resin clay. Image transfer on clay is quite versatile. For other variations using this technique, images applied to clay may be used to imitate painted porcelain or old tintype photos.

Scrimshaw Pendant

Designed by Rachel Haab

WHAT YOU'LL NEED

- Ruler
- Staple bezel (Objects and Elements)
- Black-and-white image printed on glossy photo laser-printer paper
- Gloves
- KlayResin in Porcelain White (Sherri Haab Designs)
- Spoon
- Cup or small bowl of water
- Craft knife
- Acrylic paint in brown, black, ivory, or light yellow
- Cloth
- Wire cutters
- 22- to 24-gauge wire, approximately 3 inches (7.5cm)
- Chain-nose pliers
- Round-nose pliers
- Chain (Vintaj)
- Various beads
- Jump rings (Vintaj)

1. Measure the inside dimensions of your bezel. Cut out a toner-based image printed with a laser printer matching these dimensions. We used an image printed with black toner for an authentic scrimshaw look, but a color copy would also work.

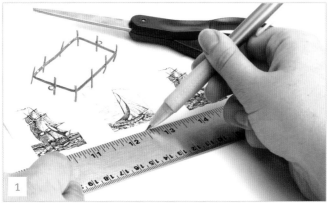

2. Test-fit your cut-out image in the bezel. The image should fit nicely within the boundaries of the bezel without scraping its edges.

3. Wearing gloves, knead the resin and catalyst together to a uniform color. Working quickly, create a flat pad of clay, then press it onto the printed image. Using the shape of the cut-out image as a guide, gently work the clay into the correct shape and dimensions. The piece should be at least ³⁄₁₆ inch (5mm) thick for strength.

4. Burnish the paper with the back of a spoon to ensure that the image will adhere well to the clay. Let the piece cure for at least 30 minutes.

5. Place the piece in a cup of water and let sit for 10 minutes, or until the paper becomes slightly transparent. Remove the piece and, starting in the center, slowly roll away the

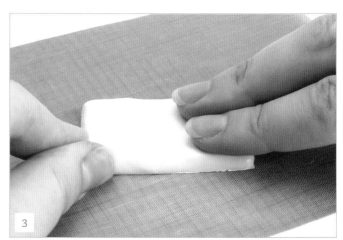

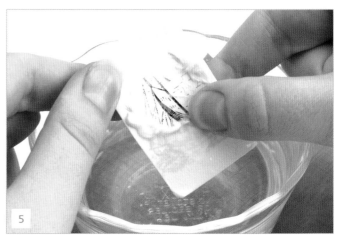

paper using your fingertips. (Beginning at the center will prevent the image from peeling up at the corners.) The paper will pull away, leaving the image embedded in the clay. Continue rubbing to remove all paper debris.

6. Drag the craft knife over the hardened clay to make scratches and faux cracks. Don't be afraid to cut through the image; this will give the surface a more authentic look.

7. Mix brown and black acrylic paint to create dark brown, then rub it over the entire piece using a paintbrush or your fingers, making sure to fill in the scratches.

8. While the paint is still wet, use a slightly damp cloth to wipe most of the paint away, leaving the scratches of the pendant stained. Let dry.

9. If desired, antique the piece again with ivory or light yellow acrylic paint, again using a damp cloth to wipe away any excess. Allow the piece to dry fully.

10. Using chain-nose pliers, bend the staples on the back of the bezel slightly inward toward its center. Place your resin clay pendant inside.

11. Secure the piece in the bezel by crimping down the staples on the front of the bezel with the pliers.

12. Add beaded wire links to connect the pendant to the chain. Refer to the section on page 37 about making wrapped wire loops. Cut a length of wire about 3 inches (7.5cm) long. Bend the wire to a 90-degree angle with chain-nose pliers, leaving a 1-inch (2.5cm) tail. Switch to round-nose pliers and then work the wire around them to form a loop.

13. Hold the loop with chain-nose pliers and wrap the end of the wire around the base of the loop a few times to secure it.

14. Clip off the excess wire and tuck the end of the wire close to the wrap with the pliers. Add a bead close to the completed wrapped section and form a loop on the other side of the bead.

15. Continue to add sections of beaded links as desired. Use jump rings to attach a clasp finding to the chain ends and to attach the finished pendant.

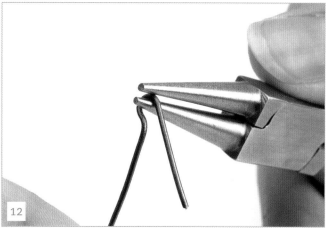

Recreating Raku

Raku ware is traditionally made with ceramic clay that's fired in organic material such as dried leaves. As the materials burn, they impart an unpredictable yet rich array of colors to the glaze. A single piece may be covered with a rainbow of hues.

The pigment powders that are applied to the resin clay in this project can be layered to mimic a raku-fired ceramic bead without the need for a kiln. KlayResin in Urban Steel is great because the neutral color simulates a dark piece of pottery under the bright colors of Pearl Ex powder. However, you can use any type of resin clay in any color you like for this project.

Raku Beads Bracelet

Designed by Sherri Haab

WHAT YOU'LL NEED

- Craft knife
- KlayResin in Urban Steel (Sherri Haab Designs)
- Gloves
- Wooden skewer
- Leather embossing stamps (Tandy Leather Factory)
- Dust mask
- Pearl Ex Powdered Pigments in assorted colors (Jacquard Products)
- Paintbrush for applying powdered pigment (optional)
- 1½ yards (1.4m) nylon or other synthetic-fiber beading cord
- 6° or size E seed beads
- Loop-and-toggle clasp
- Jewelry cement

1. Slice off a small section of the clay to make one bead at a time. Wearing gloves, knead the clay quickly until it is uniform in color.
2. Roll the clay into a ball.

3. Slide the ball onto a wooden skewer. If you're using quick-setting clay, spend only a brief time reshaping the bead.
4. Texture the bead with a leather embossing stamp that's been dipped in pigment powder. Loading the stamp with pigment not only embellishes the clay with color but keeps the stamp from sticking to the clay. Remember to wear a dust mask whenever you work with a powdered medium.
5. Press the stamp into the side of bead. Repeat your design around the entire bead, dipping the stamp into the powder as needed.
6. Remove the bead from the skewer and reshape it if it's still soft. It doesn't need to be perfect, as actual raku pottery is often organic and irregular. Once the bead is firm but still tacky, brush or rub different colors of pigment powder over

its surface. Make sure to wear a dust mask when working with dry pigment powders. Layer and combine colors to resemble the varied iridescent effects found in raku pottery. Repeat steps 1–6 to create additional beads. Let cure for 24 hours before proceeding to the next step.

7. To string the beads, cut three strands of cord each 18 inches (45.5cm) long. Tie a knot about 3 inches (7.5cm) from one end. Add seed beads along the cords, braiding them as you incorporate the beads. In this design, two beads were added between each crossover of the cords to form the braid. Add a raku clay bead with a knot formed with all three cords to secure each side of the bead. Continue the braided pattern between each clay bead until you're happy with the length.

8. To finish, tie one element of the clasp finding to each end with a knot.

9. Tie three seed beads to the end of each cord, securing them with a knot under each bead. Clip the cord close to the knot and finish the end with jewelry cement to prevent fraying.

Faux Coral

Coral as a jewelry-making material is often avoided by eco-conscious designers who are concerned about harming these endangered marine organisms. Fortunately, resin clay can be shaped and polished to mimic coral branches and beads. Real coral is available in many colors, including red, pink, white, black, blue, and violet, all of which can be re-created with resin clay. Apoxie Sculpt clay comes in bright, saturated colors, so this clay is perfect for imitating the strong colors of coral. Other clays can be used to create this project as well.

Form the coral branches fairly thick for strength. After the piece cures, buffing the surface will add a sheen that will enhance its natural beauty.

Coral Branch Pendant
Designed by Sherri Haab

WHAT YOU'LL NEED

- Apoxie Sculpt in red, orange, and white (Aves)
- Gloves
- Scraps of cured black clay
- Mat-cutter blade
- Small length of 22- to 24-gauge wire
- Pair of round-nose pliers
- Soft cloth or variable-speed bench lathe fitted with a muslin wheel

1. Wearing gloves, mix small amounts of red, orange, and white two-part resin clays to obtain a pleasing red coral color. Roll the clay into a small ball, then add an equal amount of catalyst, mixing thoroughly. Shape the mixed clay into a log, then pinch off thinner branch shapes that stem from the log to resemble coral.

2. Continue to refine and thin the branches of the coral design. If you're working with clay that has a long curing time, you can let it sit for 30 minutes to firm up a bit. While you're waiting, you can chop up small bits of black clay as described in the next step.

3. To add small black specks of color to the coral, chop up some hardened bits of scrap clay with a mat-cutter blade. The dried pieces of clay will be embedded into the coral.

4. Press the chopped bits of black clay into the coral while the clay is still soft.

5. Use the wire and a pair of round-nose pliers to make a twisted loop for hanging the pendant, then embed it into the clay.

6. Continue to refine the shape as it starts to harden, curving the branch for a realistic look. Let the clay cure overnight.

7. To add a soft gloss finish to the coral clay, buff the cured clay with a soft cloth until the surface has a smooth sheen. Alternatively, you can buff with a mechanical wheel of a bench lathe at a slow speed using a muslin wheel (see page 21).

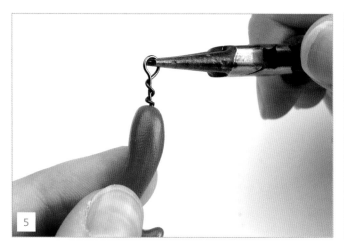

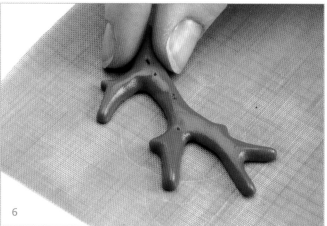

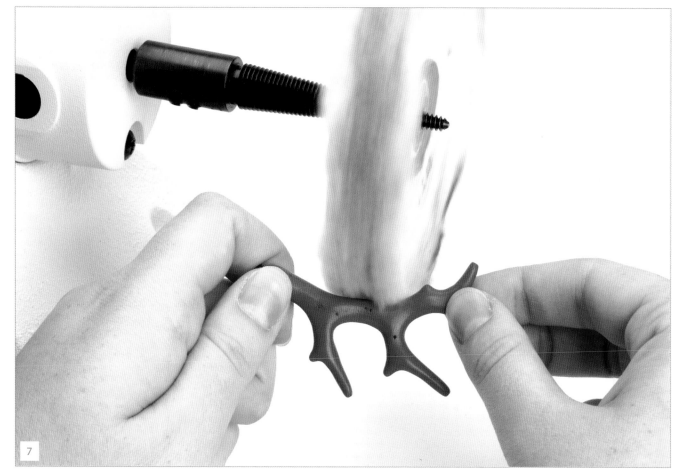

Authentic Metallic Effects

These faux copper bracelets are formed directly on your own wrist as they cure for a perfect fit! Because KlayResin cures so quickly, it only takes a few minutes for it to become rigid. Just make sure to leave enough space between the two ends of your cuff bracelet—at least 1½ inches (3.8cm)—so you can take it off after it hardens. Play around with different textures, embellishments, and sizes to make a variety of interesting, one-of-a-kind cuffs. KlayResin is a great base for the metallic effect in these bracelets because the clay itself has a slight metallic shine. The faux-copper clay was enhanced by brushing a shiny metallic acrylic paint onto the high areas of the textured piece. This technique can be used to create a metallic finish for any color of clay. For a variation, you can embellish your cuff with a small decorative object, such as a coin or charm cast from an original piece (see Molding Scrap Clay, page 104).

Copper Cuff Bracelet
Designed by Rachel Haab

WHAT YOU'LL NEED

- Gloves
- KlayResin in Rustic Copper (Sherri Haab Designs)
- Plastic clay roller
- Craft knife
- Rubber stamps for texturing

- Olive oil
- Coin or other charm for decoration (optional)
- Rubber-tipped clay shaper tool (optional)
- Acrylic paint in copper, blue-green, and/or black

- Paintbrush for acrylic paint
- Soft cloth
- Water-based varnish
- Paintbrush for water-based varnish

1. Wearing gloves, knead together the two parts of the clay until the mixture is fully uniform with no marbling. Working quickly, roll out a thick rope of clay.
2. Use the roller to flatten the rope. Create a flat sheet of clay in the desired width and length of your cuff bracelet. If necessary, use a craft knife to trim away any excess clay. Straighten and refine the edges using your fingertips, rounding the ends of the piece so the cuff will be comfortable and have no sharp edges.
3. Brush the rubber stamp with olive oil, then use it to texture the clay by pressing it into the surface.
4. Pick up the flat piece of clay and mold it into shape by wrapping it around your wrist. Leave at least 1½ inches (3.8cm) of space between the two ends of the cuff so you can remove it easily. Use your other hand to hold the shape of the bracelet around your wrist for a few minutes until the clay is cured enough to hold its own shape. Remove the bracelet from your arm.
5. Mix a small ball of clay and press it onto the center of the cuff bracelet.
6. Press your coin or other charm into the center of the ball so that it adheres to the bracelet.
7. Use your fingers or a clay shaper tool to press the ball of clay snugly around the coin. Smooth and even out the clay as you work your way around the coin, which will create a tight bezel for the coin to sit in.
8. Before the clay hardens, quickly press a rubber stamp around the bezel to create texture around the coin. Let the cuff cure completely.
9. Apply a coat of copper acrylic paint to the clay portion of the cuff to create a shiny finish. Let dry.

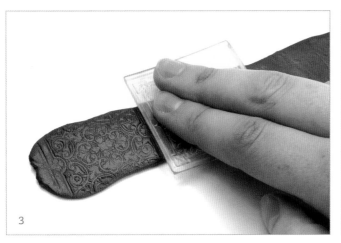

10. For a verdigris effect, apply blue-green acrylic paint to the clay, then remove it with a soft, damp cloth, leaving it in the recesses of the textured areas. This process can also be done with black acrylic to achieve an aged look. Let dry. To protect the painted surface of the bracelet, apply a coat of water-based varnish. Let dry.

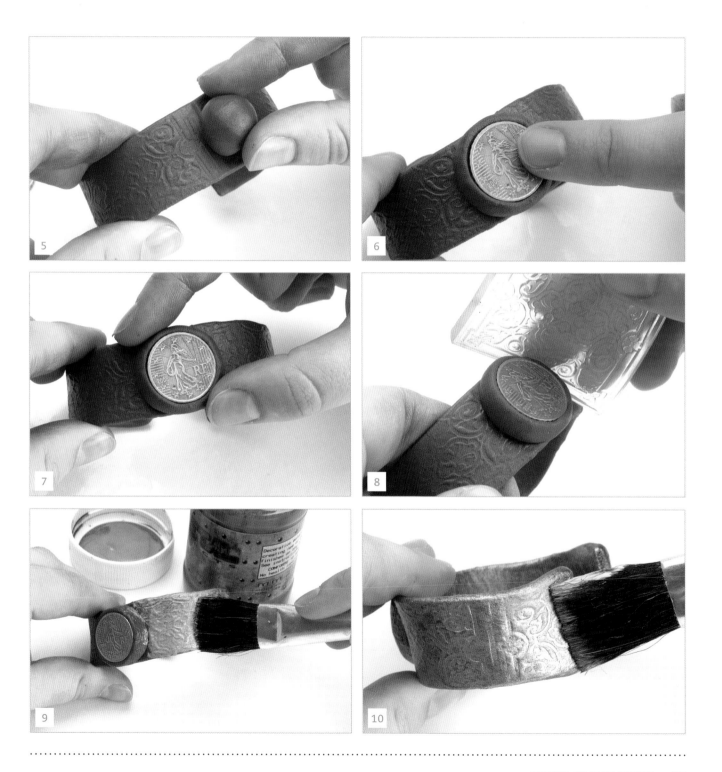

GALLERY: IMITATIVE EFFECTS

1. Concrete Earrings by Sherri Haab. Concrete KlayResin, vintage crystals, and sterling ear wires. *Photo by the artist.*

2. Red, Orange, and Blue Necklace by Alita Porter. Lumina Clay, alcohol inks, mica powder, and copper wire. *Photo by the artist.*

3. Faux Painted Porcelain Jewelry by Sherri Haab. Porcelain White KlayResin, toner image transfer, silver-plated bracelet with bezel setting, brass setting with chain. *Photo by the artist.*

4. Building an Architectural Style Necklace by Melanie Brooks. Rustic Copper KlayResin, hardware parts, metal findings, metallic powder, and sterling silver. *Photo by the artist.*

5. Black Pearl by Denise Baldwin. Aves Apoxie Clay, oyster shell, vintage earring, and Pearl Ex Powder. *Photo by the artist.*

6. Jade Pendant by Cassy Muronaka. Makin's Clay. *Photo by the artist.*

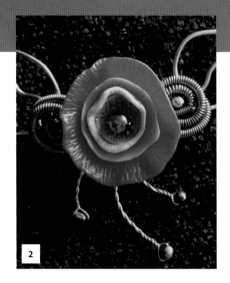

Creating Bezels

In jewelry making, the term "bezel" is used to refer to a setting for a gem or stone cabochon. It's usually a metal rim that surrounds and protects the edge of the stone. The bezel can be simple or decorative. Functionally, a bezel provides a way to securely attach a stone to a pendant or ring. Bezel findings are sold in bead shops and through jewelry-making suppliers and have become very popular with jewelry makers. Jewelry artists fill bezels with stones, resin, images, and other found objects. Resin clay can also be used to fill bezels for a variety of techniques, such as making faux stones, or it can be used as a colored adhesive to embed small beads or crystals. One example of resin which was used as an adhesive is the Clover Charm Pendant project on page 60. Because resin clay acts as an adhesive, the glass cabochon will stay put in a bezel.

Not only can resin clay fill a bezel, but it can serve as the bezel itself. Since bezels are traditionally made of metal, resin clay is a unique material to use for a bezel. Resin clay is strong and colorful, and provides an artistic solution to set cabochons or other objects. By simply surrounding your cabochon or gem with a rope of resin clay you have an instant setting. Because the clay shrinkage is minimal and there is no need to bake the clay, resin clay bezels allow many design options.

The possibilities for both filling bezels and making bezels with resin clay are endless. Techniques for using bezels include sculptural designs, creating open-backed bezels, using pigment and metal powders, and giving traditional stone settings a modern twist.

Making a Simple Bezel

One of the wonderful properties of resin clay is that it sticks to almost anything, which makes it great for creating quick-and-easy bezels around found objects.

Any clay can be used to create a simple bezel such as the one in this project. In this piece, we used Apoxie Sculpt because it is smooth and easy to use, and comes in great pre-made colors. This pendant features a glass cabochon that magnifies a brass stamping of a clover set into the clay. A brass stamping is a flat metal ornament that can be found in bead shops and craft stores. Because heat isn't required to cure the clay, a clear acrylic cabochon can be used instead. Use your own favorite trinket and wear your lucky charm wherever you go.

Clover Charm Pendant

Designed by Sherri Haab

WHAT YOU'LL NEED

- Gloves
- Apoxie Sculpt (Aves)
- Ruler
- Clover brass stamping
- Clear glass or acrylic cabochon from a bead store, or a flat glass marble from a floral supplier

- Two brass filigree bead caps
- Texturing tool (such as flat filigree)
- Paintbrush for powdered pigment
- Pearl Ex Powdered Pigment in Brilliant Gold (Jacquard Products)

- 3 inches (7.5cm) of 24-gauge half-hard brass wire
- Flat-nose pliers
- Round-nose pliers
- Cotton swab
- Rubbing alcohol
- Faceted bead for bead dangle on pendant
- Head pin

1. Knead together the two-part resin clay to a uniform color. Mold the clay into a flat circle shape, about ¼ inch (6mm) larger in diameter than the glass cabochon and ⅜ inch (9mm) thick.

2. Lightly press the brass stamping into the center of the clay shape.

3. Top the brass stamping with the glass or acrylic cabochon.

4. Begin working the clay around the perimeter of the circle and up the sides of the cabochon to create a bezel. Keep working around the entire circle to hold the cabochon in place. Leave thicker spots at the top and bottom of the bezel; these will later be used to support bead caps. Smooth and refine the edges of the bezel.

5. Press the filigree bead caps onto the top and bottom of the pendant.

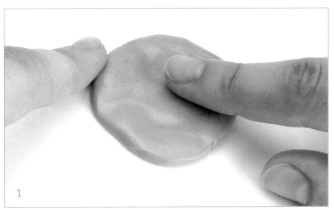

6. Create a texture around the edge of the bezel. (We've used a piece of filigree for that purpose here.)

7. Wearing a dust mask, use a paintbrush or your finger to highlight the raised texture with a light application of gold pigment powder.

8. Using the brass wire and the pliers, follow the wire-wrapping steps on page 37 to create a loop for the top of the pendant. Push the raw end of the wire loop into the hole in the bead cap, embedding it in the clay. Add a simple wire loop to the bottom of the pendant, without wrapping. Allow the piece to cure for 24 hours.

9. After the piece is fully cured, add a bead dangle to the bottom by threading a bead onto a head pin. Follow the wire-wrapping steps on page 37 to create a loop for an attachment.

Tip

Any smudges of clay or fingerprints that have transferred to the glass cabochon should be quickly wiped away with a cotton swab and rubbing alcohol.

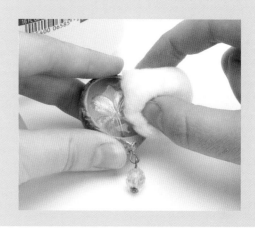

6

7

8

9

Designing an Ornate Bezel

Antique or vintage buttons can serve as beautiful and unique focal pieces for jewelry. Filigree made with thin ropes of resin clay will bond directly to a button or cabochon to create a unique ring bezel. Look at patterns in lace, wrought iron, and other filigree for inspiration to create an intricate, distinctive bezel; you can also make a simple bezel to contrast with an ornate button.

Creating an intricate filigree design usually requires a lot of time. We used Milliput Epoxy Putty for this project because it has a long working time and is a very smooth clay. This made it easy to create small, thin ropes and allowed us plenty of time to arrange them into swirls and loops around the button. Any clay with a long curing time can be used.

Filigree Button Ring
Designed by Rachel Haab

WHAT YOU'LL NEED

‣ Gloves
‣ Milliput Epoxy Putty in Black (Milliput)

‣ Antique or vintage button with a shank
‣ Teflon sheet

‣ MultiMandrel (Metal Clay Supply)
‣ Cellophane tape
‣ Craft knife (optional)

1. Wearing gloves, knead together the two-part resin clay to a uniform color with no marbling. Roll a small amount of clay into a ball, then press it into the back of the button to cover the shank.

2. Work your way around the base of the button, pressing the ball of clay to adhere it to the back of the button and smoothing any rough edges. Use your finger to flatten the bottom of the clay ball to create a level base.

3. Roll out a thin rope of clay to use for your filigree.

4. Stick one end of the rope to the clay below the button. Begin to create loops, gently pressing the clay (without flattening it) to the surface of the button as you work.

5. It's easiest to create the filigree pattern in sections; in this example, sections of three loops each were created before the excess rope was cut away using a craft knife and a new section created. Continue this process around the circumference of the button.

6. To hide the raw edges of rope in the filigree, create tiny balls of clay and gently press them over any raw edges, creating a pattern as you work your way around the button. Set aside.

7. Roll a rope of clay for the ring shank.

8. Wrap a small scrap of the Teflon sheet around a ring mandrel in the preferred ring size and secure with cellophane tape. This will protect your mandrel and keep your ring from sticking to the surface. Wrap the clay rope around the Teflon on the mandrel.

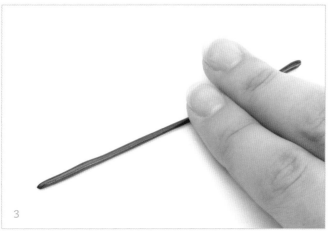

9. Blend the seam using your fingers. This section of ring will be hidden underneath your button, so it doesn't need to be perfect.

10. Press your fingers around the rope of clay to gather and flatten any extra clay in a pad at the top of the ring, where it will help the button adhere more securely.

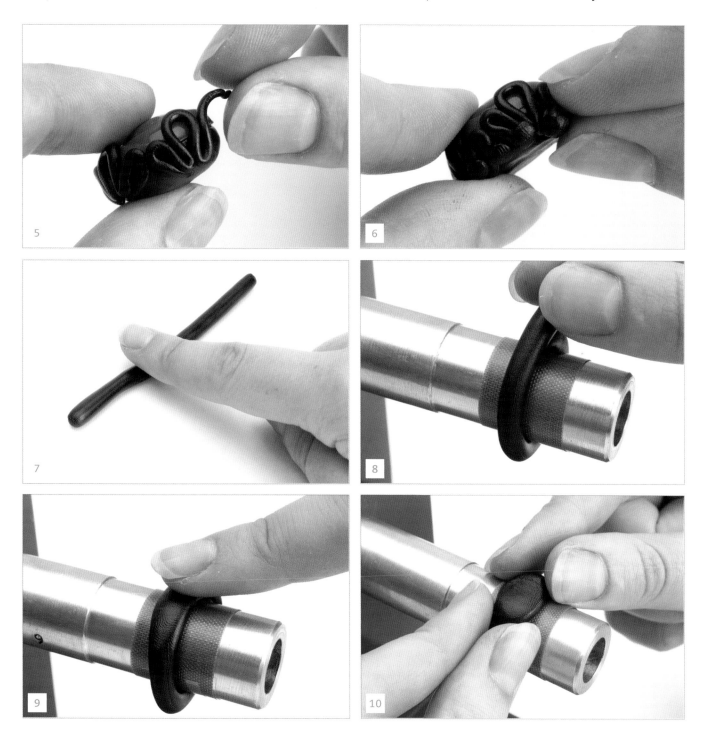

11. Press the button onto the flattened pad of clay so the two parts adhere.

12. Refine and smooth out any imperfections, then let cure fully.

Making a Backless Bezel

Combining liquid resin and resin clay is an interesting way to contrast the transparent with the opaque, and the delicate with the strong, in one jewelry piece. This technique uses resin clay to create bezel frames into which colorful epoxy resin is poured. Any clay with a moderately long working time is needed for time to cut out and refine these little resin clay frames. Apoxie Sculpt is a great choice because it comes in great colors and gives you the perfect amount of time before curing. Any colorant suitable for liquid resin can be used, but we used oil paint because of the smooth, semitransparent color it yields. The project shown presents a stained-glass look in a simple geometric shape, but the same technique can be used to create opaque and organic-looking pieces such as seascapes, floral designs, and lace patterns.

Stained-Glass Earrings
Designed by Rachel Haab

WHAT YOU'LL NEED

- Gloves
- Apoxie Sculpt in Black (Aves)
- Teflon sheet
- Plastic clay roller
- Craft knife
- Needle tool or toothpick

- Rubber-tipped clay shaper
- Packing tape
- EnviroTex Lite Pour On Epoxy Resin
- Waxed paper
- Wooden toothpicks and mixing cups (for mixing the liquid resin)

- Oil paints in various colors
- Jump rings
- Chain-nose pliers
- Ear wires

1. Wearing gloves, knead together the resin and catalyst clay to a uniform color with no marbling. Using the Teflon sheet as a working surface, roll the clay out into a thin sheet, about ⅛ to ¼ inch (3- to 6mm) thick.
2. Cut out the desired earring shapes with the craft knife. This can be done freehand, or you can create a paper pattern to trace around to ensure that your earrings are the same size. Remove any excess clay.
3. Pierce the top of each earring with a needle tool to make a hole to attach the earring hook later. Make the hole close to the top of the earring so a jump ring can fit through it but don't make the hole so close to the edge that the frame is weakened. In this piece, the hole is a little less than ⅛ inch (3mm) from the top.

4. To create the frame, cut out the inside of the earring shapes, keeping the cut parallel to the outer edge of the earring. Be sure to leave ample space around the hole at the top of the earring for stability. Don't worry if the earring becomes slightly stretched during this process, it can be reshaped later. Remove the excess clay.

5. If needed, reshape the earrings at this point by gently pushing the frame with your fingers or a rubber-tipped clay shaper. Next, use the shaper to smooth out the edges of the frame. Work your way around the inside and outside edges of each earring, pushing in any ragged edges. Let the clay cure completely.

6. Once the earrings have cured, remove them from the Teflon and press a piece of packing tape to the back of each frame. Because the tape will act as the barrier when the liquid resin is poured into the frame, you should use your fingernail to press the tape down to ensure a good seal. Fold the two ends of the tape in on itself to give you something to hold on to on the edge.

7. Mix the liquid resin according to the manufacturer's instructions. For these earrings, about 10cc (10ml, or 2 teaspoons) of resin was used.

8. Drop a little bit of the liquid resin onto waxed paper, then use a toothpick to color it with a very small amount of oil paint. Mix the paint and the resin thoroughly.

4

5

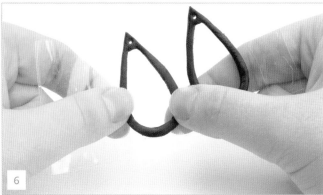
6

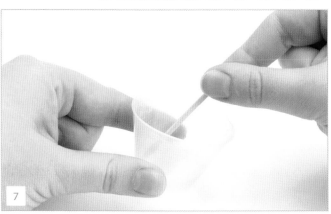
7

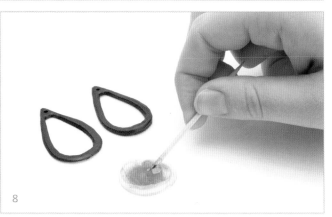
8

9. Use a toothpick to drop resin into the lower section of each frame. To prevent dripping, dip the toothpick into the resin and then roll the toothpick in your fingers as you lift and transfer the resin. This rolling motion will keep the resin balled up on the end of the stick. Continue adding resin in this manner until you have the right amount.

10. Repeat step 8 to create a second color, then drop this color into the upper section of the frame. Add more until the resin is level with the top of the frame.

11. If desired, use a toothpick to blend the two colors together to form a gradient. Let the liquid resin cure overnight.

12. Once the liquid resin has cured, gently remove the packing tape from the back of each earring.

13. Thread a jump ring through the hole at the top of an earring, then slide on an ear wire. Close the jump ring. Repeat for the second earring.

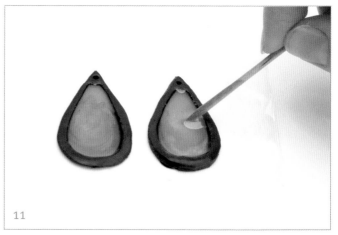

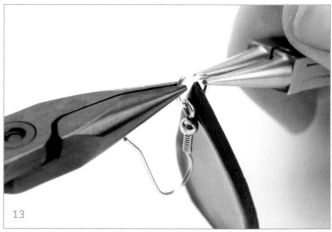

Designing an Organic Bezel

When we found gorgeous, tiny geodes at a bead show, we felt they just had to be made into jewelry! We were inspired to use a metal ring blank as a base to secure the geode as we built a resin clay bezel directly around its organic shape. We then embellished the clay with metallic powder to create the effect of brushed metal. For this project, it is good to use a clay that is similar in color to the metallic powder you choose to coat it with. This way, if any of the clay shows through after you paint on the powder, it won't be noticeable. Apoxie Sculpt had a great color for this project and a long working time, which is needed for refining the piece and allowing time for painting on the metallic powder onto the wet clay.

This technique can also be used with any type of rock or natural stone, including pyrite (also known as fool's gold) or crystals.

Geode Ring
Designed by Michelle Haab

WHAT YOU'LL NEED

- Adjustable metal ring blank (Sherri Haab Designs)
- Chain-nose pliers
- Waxed paper
- Two-part epoxy adhesive (quick-setting)
- Toothpick

- Small geode or other irregularly shaped stone or rock
- Gloves
- Apoxie Sculpt (Aves)
- Dust mask
- Paintbrush for applying the metallic powder

- Metallic powder
- Plastic clay roller
- Paintbrush for applying varnish
- Water-based varnish
- Craft knife (optional)

1. Pull apart an adjustable metal ring blank until it fits very loosely on your finger. The ring blank will provide the framework for the ring, so make sure there's enough space inside it for your finger plus a thin layer of resin clay.

2. Use a pair of chain-nose pliers to refine the ring blank into a large circle.

3. On a sheet of waxed paper, mix some quick-setting epoxy adhesive according to the package instructions.

4. Use a toothpick to drop the epoxy onto the flat pad of the ring blank.

5. Press the base of the geode onto the ring blank. Pinch the ring with your index finger behind the ring blank and your thumb against the flat side of the geode to ensure that the glue dries with the geode straight up and down. Even if your geode isn't flat on the bottom, the epoxy glue is strong enough to hold even a very curved edge. The epoxy will take

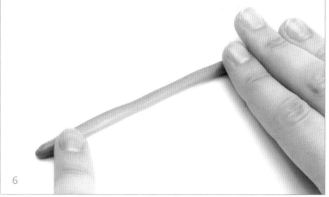

a few minutes to set, so hold the geode in place while the glue dries.

6. Wearing gloves, knead together the two parts of the resin clay to a uniform color with no marbling. Roll out a thin rope of clay.

7. Press the rope of clay around the perimeter of the ring blank. Remove any excess with a craft knife or your fingers.

8. Pinch the rope of clay around the ring blank to cover the metal. Use your fingers to blend the seam and refine the ring's shape.

9. Flatten the clay by pinching it between your fingers. It may be useful to carefully try on the ring at this point to make sure that the clay's been flattened enough to ensure a good fit.

10. Place the ring facedown on your work surface. Wearing a dust mask, brush on the metallic powder. Be sure to coat the entire surface of the ring. Let the ring cure.

11. After the clay has cured, mix up another small portion of resin clay. Use a flat circle of clay to cover the back of the ring blank, blending it up into the geode and into the already powdered ring.

12. Roll out a rope with the remaining resin clay, then use a roller to flatten the rope. Wrap this thin sheet of clay around the geode to create a bezel. Remove any excess clay with a craft knife or your fingers.

13. Blend the seams in the clay with your fingers and press the walls of the bezel up and around the flat surface of the geode, so that the top of the clay is level with the geode. Refine the shape of the bezel and press it snugly around the geode.

14. Place the ring facedown on your work surface. Wearing a dust mask, brush the metallic powder onto the wet clay. Let the clay cure.

15. Using a paintbrush, seal the ring with a coat of water-based varnish. Let dry.

GALLERY: CREATING BEZELS

1. Frozen Windows by Melanie Brooks. Two-part resin clay, clear epoxy resin, glitter, hardware parts, beads, and sterling silver. *Photo by the artist.*

2. Button Set in Clay Bezel by Melanie Brooks. Two-part resin clay, ceramic button, and sterling silver. *Photo by the artist.*

3. Trilobite Pendants by Melanie Brooks. Two-part resin clay, ceramic beads, and leather cord. *Photo by the artist.*

4. Vintage Image Necklaces by Sherri Haab. Porcelain White KlayResin, toner image transfers, fine silver, sterling chain, beads, and epoxy resin. *Photo by the artist.*

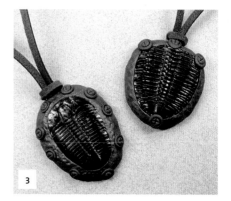

·····················

Mixing Resin Clay with Other Mediums

Resin clay can be combined with many materials and lends itself to many art techniques. By combining it with other materials, the possibilities are endless. Using a variety of art supplies such as paints, stains, foils, powders, and embedded inclusions, you can transform the clay body entirely, giving more opportunity for the same clay to be used for diverse purposes. One popular example of an art form that combines resin clay with other media is making realistic foods and desserts for display or miniatures for dollhouses. The resin clay is combined with various acrylic mediums, liquid resins, and small parts that replicate the texture of the food. This is just one common use for a mixed media application; there are so many more.

Familarize yourself with the various properties of the types of resin clay brands to know which clay is best suited for your design. For example, if you want to create a beaded mosaic design, it would be wise to choose slow-curing clay. If you would like to apply surface color, a good choice would be clay with a rough surface texture that would allow the paint to adhere evenly. Slow cure or quick, rough or smooth, each type of clay has attributes one might find appealing for one use or another.

Resin clay can be adapted to feature a preferred medium or artistic style. If you're an illustrator or painter, resin clay makes a good base for surface design techniques featuring paint, pencil, or toner. If you prefer carving, sanding, or drilling, you may do so after it is cured. So whether your talent is sculpting or getting out power tools, there's a technique for you.

Embedding Beads and Mosaics

osaic jewelry can be intricate and beautiful, but creating traditional mosaics is usually time-consuming. With this technique, the process is simplified by using a string of seed beads that are all laid into the resin clay "grout" at once, instead of placing each piece individually. The key to this technique is planning ahead: Sketch out your design as a simple line drawing, and string your beads in strands prior to mixing the resin clay. This will allow you to embed the beads quickly and give you extra time to refine the piece while the clay is still soft. For this project, you need as much working time as you can get with the clay in order to place all of your seed beads and arrange your design. Milliput has the longest curing time out of any of the resin clays and comes in a fantastic white "grout" color.

Bead Mosaic Pendant
Designed by Rachel Haab

WHAT YOU'LL NEED

- Paper and pencil
- Metal bezel (Nunn Design)
- Seed beads in various colors
- Tape
- Thread
- Beading needle
- Gloves
- Milliput Epoxy Putty in White (Milliput Company)
- Toothpick or needle tool
- Scissors
- Blunt or flat end of a tool

1. On a sheet of paper, draw a design to fit your bezel. Choose seed beads to create your mosaic. Fold a piece of tape on the end of the thread to create a stopper, then use the beading needle to string the seed beads. Each strand should be a different color, which will allow you to work more quickly when you're ready to set them into the clay. Set the bead strands aside.

2. Wearing gloves, knead together the two parts of the clay to a uniform color with no marbling. Press the clay into the bezel, filling it only about halfway because the seed beads will displace clay when they're pressed into it, which will fill the bezel the rest of the way.

3. Using your drawing as a guide, sketch your design in the clay with a toothpick or needle tool. It's easiest to do this by lightly piercing the clay with the toothpick to create a series of dots rather than dragging the toothpick through the clay.

4. Take a string of seed beads and lay it into the clay along one of the design lines. Make sure the beads are spaced evenly.

5. Working from the end of the string forward, firmly press the beads into the clay using your fingertip. When one string of beads is pressed in, cut away the tape at the end of the thread, then pull out the thread, leaving the beads embedded in the clay.

6. To create circular shapes, such as the berries in this design, loop the strand of beads in a circle by pulling the ends of the string in opposite directions. Press the beads into place, then remove the string.

7. For smaller areas, use the beading needle as a placement tool by threading a few beads onto the end of the needle and pressing them into place.

8. Repeat steps 4–7 until the design is complete. Press down each bead with the blunt or flat end of a tool to make sure they're all firmly in place. Let the piece cure fully.

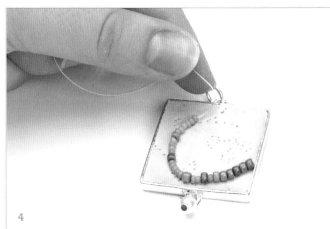

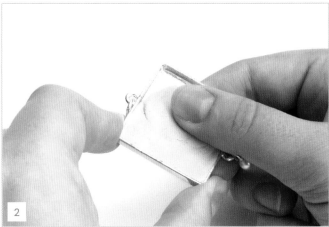

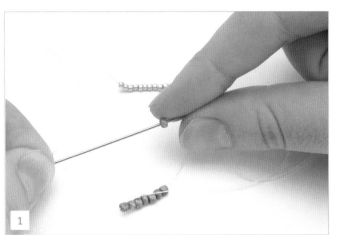

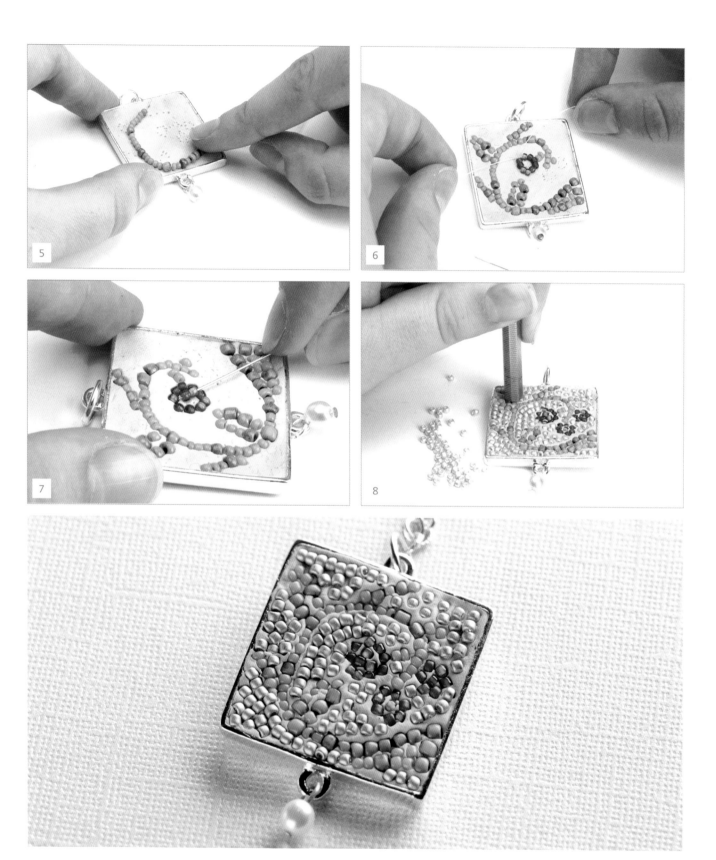

Embellishing with Colored Pencils

In this technique, we used colored pencils on concrete-look resin clay to simulate spray-painted graffiti art. We used blunt pencils in a circular motion to create the look of lighter sprays, and sharpened ones to make strong black outlines and white shadows. Get inspired by looking up work by graffiti artists on the Internet, or take inspiration from your own city. The Concrete Gray KlayResin we used here is the only clay that comes in a concrete color with actual aggregate in the clay. We used this clay to simulate concrete beneath the graffiti. You can also use colored pencils on other colors of resin clay to create geometric, floral, and other designs. Though the bangle in this project looks heavy, it's surprisingly light—we used a cardboard tube from a roll of tape as the base!

Graffiti Bracelet
Designed by Rachel Haab

WHAT YOU'LL NEED

- Empty cardboard tube from a roll of packing tape
- Craft knife or scissors
- Packing tape
- Gloves
- KlayResin in Concrete Gray (Sherri Haab Designs)
- 600-grit wet/dry sandpaper
- Pencil
- Colored pencils (Crayola or Prismacolor)
- Paintbrush for varnish
- Water-based varnish

1. An empty cardboard packing-tape roll is used as the base for this bangle. Start by pulling any leftover tape off the roll. If the roll is too large for your wrist, make it smaller by cutting away a section of the cardboard and using packing tape to tape the two cut ends together. Set aside.

2. Knead together the two parts of the clay to a uniform color with no marbling. The tube can be covered in sections, so mix up just as much clay as you feel comfortable working with. Working quickly, press out a flat pad of clay approximately the width of the cardboard tube.

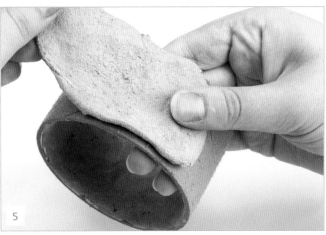

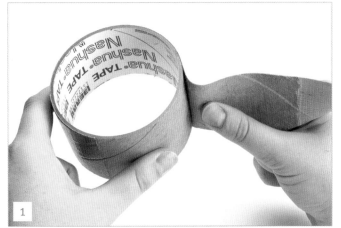

3. Line the inside of the cardboard tube with the rolled-out clay. Use your fingers to press the sheet of clay against the cardboard and to smooth the surface. Keep the edge of the clay flush with the edge of the tube.

4. Repeat steps 2 and 3 to line the remainder of the inside of the cardboard tube. Use your fingertip to blend the new section of clay into the already hardened portions of clay for a smooth finish.

5. When the inside of the tube has been covered, begin working on the outside, pressing out a thin pad of clay, this time slightly wider than the bangle so that the excess clay can be wrapped around the edge of the inside of the bracelet. Press the clay along the outside of the bangle to cover the cardboard.

6. Press the excess clay around the edge of the cardboard and blend the fresh clay with dried clay on the inside of the tube.

7. Repeat steps 5 and 6 until the tube is entirely covered in clay. Smooth out any large bumps or rough areas with your fingers as you work.

8. Set the bangle aside until the clay is fully cured. To smooth out any rough areas and to hide any unblended seams, use 600-grit wet/dry sandpaper to sand the piece with water. When you're finished sanding, rinse the bangle in water and let it dry.

9. Using a pencil, lightly sketch out your graffiti design on the bangle. Use colored pencils to draw your design directly on the bangle. Use small circular motions to create a soft, spray-painted look, and layer different colors to yield a rich, deep color or blend.

10. When you've finished drawing your design, lightly brush away any excess crumbs of colored pencil wax from the bangle. Carefully brush on a water-based varnish to protect the bracelet. Let dry.

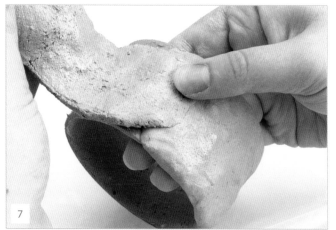

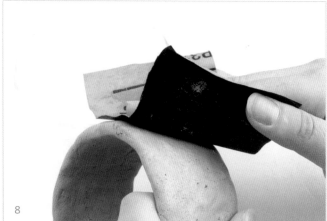

Creating a Smooth Inlay

Jewelry designer Robert Dancik works with a variety of materials to create meaningful jewelry pieces. Each creation is thoughtfully constructed by combining carefully chosen materials that work aesthetically to convey an idea or expression. With this technique, he uses resin clay to create strong graphic elements by backfilling recessed areas in a foundation of Faux Bone, then sanding the cured surface to meld the materials. Milliput is a very strong clay and can stand up to the pressure of sanding and buffing. For durability, only a two-part resin clay should be used in this project. The pendant is finished by distressing and aging the plastics to replicate the organic look and feel of real bone.

Resin Clay Inlay Pendant
Designed by Robert Dancik

WHAT YOU'LL NEED

- ¼-inch-thick (6mm-thick) sheet of Faux Bone (Robert's Real Faux Bone)
- Permanent marker
- Special Faux Bone™ saw blade in Medium or Fine and jeweler's saw frame
- Bench pin
- Electric or hand drill
- Gloves

- Milliput Epoxy Putty in black (Milliput Company)
- Metal file or flexible shaft tool and barrel sander attachment
- 320-, 400-, and 600-grit wet/dry sandpaper
- Soft cloth or buffer and unstitched muslin buffing wheel (optional)

- Tools for texturing Faux Bone; for example a checkering file, small drill bit, or craft knife
- Acrylic paint in black
- Damp cloth
- 6 inches (15cm) of wire, any gauge
- Cyanoacrylate glue (Zap-a-Gap)
- Chain or cord for the pendant

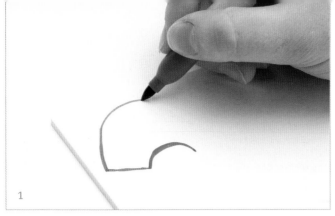

1

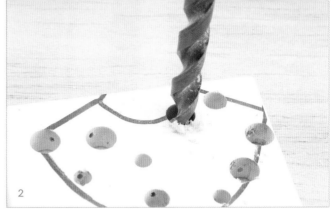

2

3

4

5

6

1. On a ¼-inch-thick (6mm) piece of Faux Bone, draw the shape of your pendant with a permanent marker.

2. Drill holes with large drill bits in the design before you cut it out. Alternatively, you could pierce shapes in the pendant for inlaying.

3. Mix the clay according to the package directions and press it into the holes. Rolling the clay into thin coils then running the coils into the holes and pressing from both sides does this most easily. Let cure.

4. Cut out your design along the drawn lines using a jeweler's saw fitted with a fine or medium blade. Use a bench pin clamped to a table to steady the work as you saw.

5. File the clay down to the surface of the Faux Bone. File to round the edges and give the piece more dimension. (The barrel sander on a flex shaft is excellent for inside curves and various other sanding operations.)

6. Sand the entire piece with wet/dry sandpaper and water, starting with 320 grit, progressing to 400 grit, and finishing

7

8

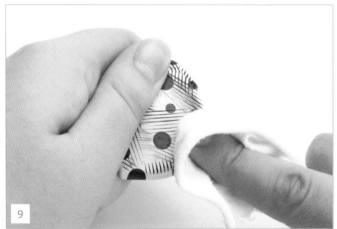

9

10

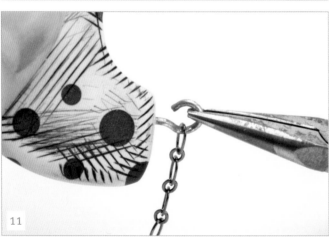

11

a checkering file to make a series of parallel lines; on the other, he used a small drill bit to make tiny dots around the larger dots of inlayed epoxy clay.) Even a craft knife can be used to scratch lines into the pendant.

8. Rub the entire piece with black acrylic paint, then let dry slightly.

9. Rub off excess paint with a damp cloth, with your fingers, or by sanding lightly with 600-grit sandpaper. Use a soft cloth or an unstitched muslin wheel to polish the piece one last time.

10. Fashion eye pins from any wire you like. Drill a hole in your pendant the same size as the wire and where you want to attach a chain or cord. Scratch the wire with a file. Put a bit of cyanoacrylate glue on the tip of the wire and inject the wire into the hole; as you do this, the glue will wick into the hole and anchor it securely.

11. Attach the finished pendant to a chain or cord.

with 600 grit. After the last sanding, turn the 600-grit sand-paper over to the paper side and rub the piece vigorously to a satin sheen. Rub the piece in the palm of your hand to get a bit of your skin's oil on the piece, then rub it on a soft cloth to bring it to a polished finish. Alternatively, after the sanding you can buff the piece on an unstitched muslin buffing wheel with no compound on it.

7. After polishing, mark the surface using any number of tools. (On one side Robert used a texturing tool called

Creating Realistic Food

You can replicate tiny dollhouse-scale desserts using lightweight air-dry clays such as Makin's Clay. Any resin clay can be used to create cute mini foods. We used Makin's Clay because it has a fluffy texture and a matte finish that makes it perfect for simulating the consistency of cakes and ice cream. Makin's also comes in many colors, which can be mixed to create realistic hues for food.

By adding paints, liquid resin, and acrylic mediums you can make them look like the real thing. Hobby shops that carry supplies for model trains and dollhouses have small dishes and accessories that are fun to use in conjunction with the clay. Little doilies, parfait dishes, and cake platters add charm to adorable little treats.

Creating imitative foods with air-dry clay is popular in Japan; trained artisans reproduce everything from miniature pastries to actual-sized restaurant menu samples that are hard to discern from the real thing.

Desserts and Pastry Treats
Designed by Sherri Haab

WHAT YOU'LL NEED

- Makin's Clay in various colors—primary and pastel colors, white, and shades of brown (Makin's)
- Needle tool
- Mat-cutter blade
- Several small paintbrushes for applying paints and varnish

- Acrylic tube paints in white, brown, black, and red
- Soft cloths
- Acrylic Molding Paste (Golden)
- Waxed paper
- Toothpicks
- Dollhouse-sized dishes (or make your own with clay)

- Acrylic gloss medium
- Two-part epoxy adhesive (quick-setting)
- Red oil paint
- Rubber-tipped clay shaper
- Acrylic gel medium
- Glass glitter (for pastries and doughnuts, optional)
- Water-based varnish

ICE CREAM SUNDAES

1. Make ice cream scoops by shaping small balls of pastel-colored clay. To make strawberry, mix light pink with red bits of clay streaked through. If you drag your finger over the ball, it will give the ice cream a realistic look. You don't want it perfectly smooth; it should appear as though a scoop scraped the surface.

2. To make mint chocolate chip ice cream, mix light green and add tiny specks of dried dark brown clay, embedding the bits into the surface of the clay. Roll white clay to make vanilla, and mix light and dark brown to resemble peanut butter fudge or another favorite flavor with those same colors.

3. Shape a small, pale yellow piece of clay into a banana shape. Score the sides with a needle tool.

4. After the clay banana dries, use a mat-cutter blade to split the banana in half. Paint the clay with watered-down brown acrylic paint. Wipe off the paint with a cloth, leaving paint in the recessed areas.

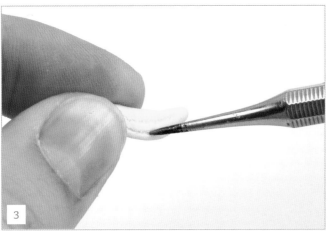

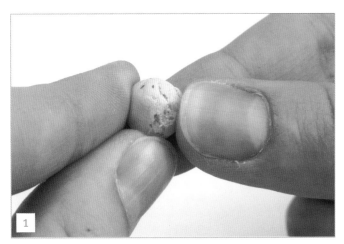

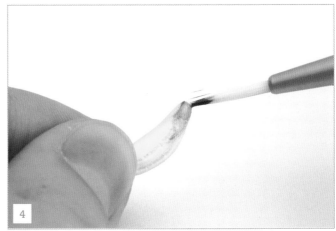

5. To make whipped cream, mix white acrylic tube paint and acrylic molding paste with a toothpick on waxed paper.

6. Use the mixed "cream" to attach the ice cream to a dollhouse-sized plate. Place the bananas on the side of the ice cream scoops using the cream as an adhesive.

7. To make fake hot fudge, mix acrylic gloss medium with black and brown acrylic paint to make a glossy paint. Drop over the ice cream scoops with a toothpick.

8. Make chopped nuts by using a mat-cutter blade to chop up fine pieces of dried light beige clay.

Tip

Make some parts in advance, such as dried pieces of clay to use for nuts, cherries, and chocolate chips. This will help them to hold a crisp shape when added to soft clay, for realistic textures and details.

5

6

7

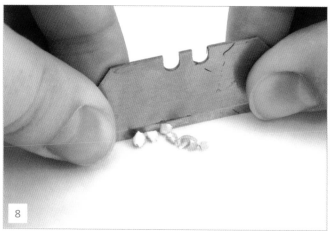

8

9. Sprinkle the chopped bits over the "fudge" gloss medium to finish the banana split.

10. For an ice cream sundae variation, mix quick-setting two-part epoxy adhesive with a very small amount of red oil paint to resemble a fruit topping. Mix well with a toothpick and then add the paint after mixing well. Drizzle over the ice cream and let cure.

9

10

DOUGHNUTS AND PASTRIES

1. For a round doughnut, mix light beige-colored clay and shape a small ball into a flattened round shape. Form a hole with a tapered needle tool, piercing all the way through and widening to enlarge the hole.

2. Decorate the doughnut with "chocolate glaze" made with dark brown acrylic paint mixed with acrylic gloss medium.

3. To make a cinnamon twist–style pastry, make two thin ropes of beige-colored clay and spiral them together to form the shape.

4. When the twist pastry is dry, add dark brown acrylic paint to the recessed areas to resemble cinnamon.

5. Use a damp cloth to remove any paint from the surface.

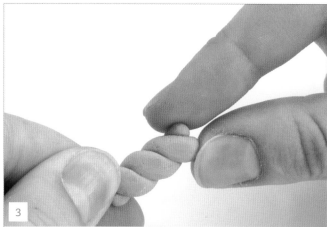

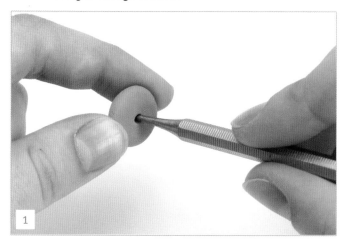

6. A maple bar doughnut is made by forming a long, flat shape, then scoring it with a needle tool to create baking rack marks on the surface. Let the shape dry and then coat the top with a warm light-brown acrylic paint mixed with gloss medium to resemble the glaze.

7. For a jelly doughnut, make a depression in the center of a flattened round piece with a rubber-tipped clay shaper tool.

8. Add a vanilla glaze to the fried doughnut shape by mixing white acrylic paint with acrylic gel medium. Sprinkle on glass glitter to resemble sugar.

9. Mix a small amount of quick-setting two-part epoxy adhesive on waxed paper with a toothpick and mix in a small speck of red oil paint for color. Drop into the center of the doughnut to complete the jelly part of the doughnut.

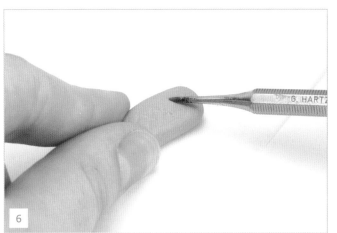

FANCY CAKE

1. Form a ball of white clay and flatten it into a cylinder shape for the cake base. Let this piece dry.

2. To add frosting rosettes to the top of the cake, begin by twisting thin ropes of white clay together.

3. Cut small sections and form them into small round rings. Roll a small ball of red to place in the center of each for a "cherry." Dry these before making the frosting for the cake.

4. To frost the cake, mix gel medium and brown acrylic paint with a toothpick on waxed paper.

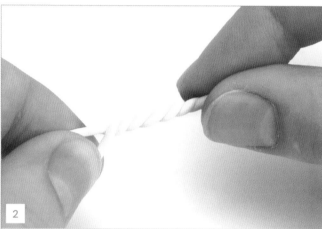

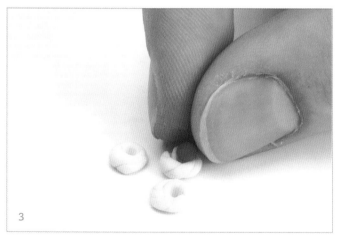

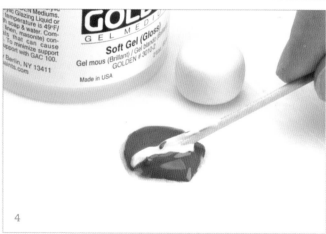

5. Spread the paint onto the cake form with a paintbrush.

6. While the paint is still wet, sprinkle chopped pieces of dried light-beige clay bits around the sides of the cake to resemble nuts. (See step 8 of Ice Cream Sundaes on page 95 for how to chop dried clay with a small mat-cutter blade.)

7. Add the cherry frosting rosettes to the top of the cake while the paint "frosting" is still wet.

8. After everything is dry, paint the cherries with water-based varnish to give them a shiny, realistic look.

GALLERY: RESIN CLAY AND OTHER MEDIUMS

1. **Different Drummer** by Leslie Blackford. Makin's Clay and acrylic paint. *Photo by the artist.*

2. **Key Keeper** by Melanie Brooks. Two-part black resin clay, hardware parts, old key, and sterling chain. *Photo by the artist.*

3. **Fake Waffles** by Osamu Watanabe. Air-dry resin clay, glass paint, and acrylic paint. *Photo by Nobuyoshi Okumura.*

Molding and Sculpting Techniques

One of the essentials of sculpting and molding is having great tools. First and foremost, your own hands are often the best for the job. Rubbing a bit of lotion or olive oil into your hands will help to prevent the clay from sticking. One thing to remember about working with your hands and resin clay is that your hands will give off heat, which can cause either sticky clay or quick curing depending on the type. Work in a cool room with most types of clay or, in the case of slow-curing types, allow the clay to rest to firm up.

Many talented artists are using resin clay to create fantastical sculptures and figurines. Sculpted figures can be as detailed as the artist can imagine. It is helpful to use armatures (such as a wire frame) inside a clay figure to give a piece form and strength. An armature can be most anything, including wire, aluminum foil, cardboard, or Styrofoam. Learn more about using Styrofoam as a core for clay in the Oversize-Bead Necklace on page 112.

There are great tools and molds available for ceramic and polymer clays that are perfect to adapt for use with resin clay. Use olive oil as a release agent to prevent molds and tools from sticking. Clean tools with rubbing alcohol shortly after using them to prevent the buildup of clay that is difficult to remove when cured.

So whether using clay for a large museum display or in a tiny dollhouse, resin clay is wonderful for replicating textured surfaces, sculpted figures, or casting from a mold to easily create a likeness of almost anything.

Molding Scrap Clay

Whenever you have leftover clay from a project, before the clay dries you can quickly use a button or nonstick mold to make medallions such as the ones shown here to add to rings. A nonstick mold may also be used if it's been coated with a release agent such as olive oil. These beautiful wax seal rings are the perfect use for scraps of clay, and any type of leftover resin clay is great for this project. These simple rings are quick and easy to make, and they're instantly beautiful! Look around for interesting textures, objects, and designs that can be molded to create them. The luster of these pieces and the textures of vintage buttons or monograms make them truly unique.

Wax Seal Ring

Designed by Rachel Haab

WHAT YOU'LL NEED

- Small piece of Teflon sheet
- MultiMandrel (MetalClay Supply)
- Cellophane tape
- Craft knife
- Any type of leftover resin clay
- Olive oil
- Woodland Arte Metal Decorivet (Vintaj), or other textured charm
- Leather stamps (Tandy Leather Factory) (optional)
- Pearl Ex Powdered Pigments (Jacquard Products)
- Paintbrush (optional)

1. Wrap a scrap of Teflon around a ring mandrel in the preferred ring size and secure with tape. This will protect your mandrel and keep your ring from sticking to the surface. Roll out a small strip of clay and trim it to the desired width using a craft knife.
2. Wrap the clay strip around the mandrel. Cut through the overlapped clay and remove the excess.
3. Blend the seam using your fingers. This section of ring will be hidden underneath your medallion, so it doesn't need to be perfect.
4. Using another piece of clay, roll out a small ball and flatten it into a circle about the size of a coin. Rub a bit of olive oil onto a Decorivet medallion or other texture to prevent sticking and press it into the circle of clay. Slowly remove the texture and gently reshape your circle if needed.
5. Press the textured clay medallion onto the ring, covering the seam. If extra adhesive is needed, use a small scrap of clay as "glue" between the ring and medallion.
6. Texture the surface of the ring with the leather stamp if desired. Wearing a dust mask, use your finger or a paintbrush to dust Pearl Ex powder over the surface of the ring and highlight the texture. Let the resin fully cure.

Using Molds to Create Texture

Using two-part silicone putty, you can make molds from many found objects. Even common items found around the house can be made into texture molds; in this project we used an old picture frame with a floral design. Use favorite charms, buttons, branches, and toys to create your own molds. The molding putty allows you to make two-part molds to create three-dimensional pieces, or you can easily create flat molds to texture your clay. The flexibility and non-stick nature of the molds make it easy to remove finished resin clay pieces. Any clay can be used in these nonstick silicone molds. We used Apoxie Sculpt for this project because of the bright color, but you can use whatever clay you like for your molded piece.

Red Rose Pendant
Designed by Michelle Haab

WHAT YOU'LL NEED

- Clear glass piece
- Collage paper or ephemera for decorating the piece
- Pencil
- Scissors
- Mod Podge (Plaid)
- Paintbrush for applying Mod Podge (Plaid)
- Two-part silicone mold putty
- Picture frame or other texture
- Apoxie Sculpt (Aves)
- Plastic clay roller
- Craft knife
- Needle tool

1. Place a glass piece on top of the collage paper and use a pencil to trace around the outside edge. Set aside the glass piece and use scissors to cut out the shape.

2. Use Mod Podge to layer pieces of collage paper with a paintbrush to create your design. Once dry, coat the front of the collage paper and press it onto the acrylic, then coat the back to seal the entire piece and let dry.

3. Combine equal portions of Part A and Part B of the mold putty and knead until a uniform color is achieved.

4. Press the mold putty onto your frame or texture surface and allow several minutes for it to set.

5. Wearing gloves, knead the resin clay using equal parts of color and the catalyst. Remove gloves and press the clay into the finished silicon mold.

6. Use the clay roller to flatten and press the clay into the mold.

7. Place the finished glass piece on top of the clay and press lightly to secure it in place.

8. Use a craft knife to cut the desired shape around the piece.

9. Roll a very thin rope out of the leftover clay and place around the acrylic piece. Cut off the excess clay and blend the seam.

10. Use the needle tool to pierce holes in the top and bottom to add chain and charm dangles if desired. Let cure. Use the wire-wrapping techniques found on page 37 to add chain and beads to the necklace. In this piece, a small key charm was added by threading a jump ring through the key and then the hole at the bottom of the pendant.

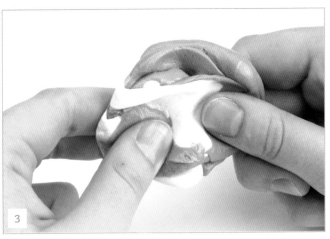

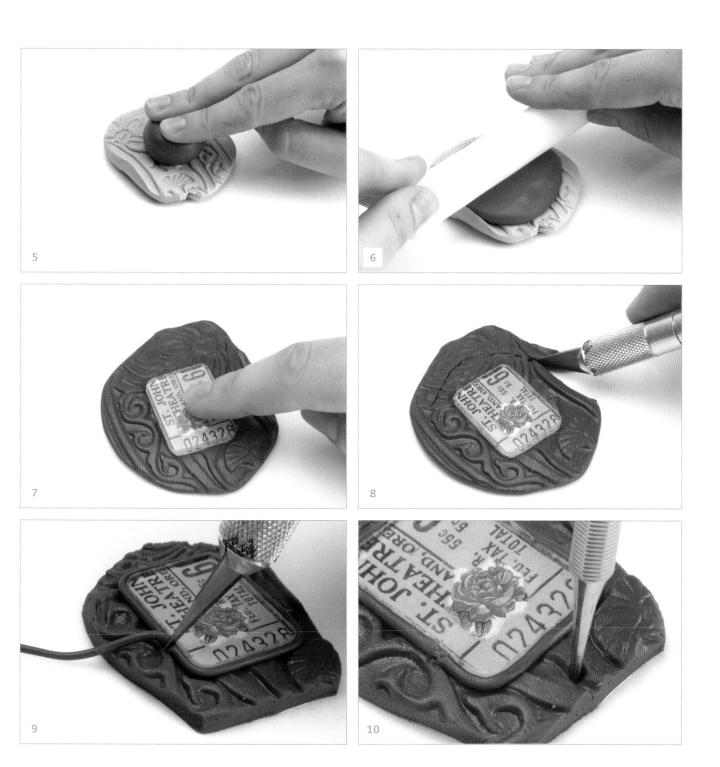

5

6

7

8

9

10

Creating Beads over Cores

Plastics, Styrofoam, and other materials that can't be heated are off-limits for use in polymer clay because it's baked in an oven. But because resin clay doesn't require baking to cure, many materials that aren't used in polymer jewelry can be utilized, thus opening up a whole new world of techniques and opportunities! Styrofoam is great as a base form in resin clay because an avant-garde, larger-than-life look can be achieved without extreme weight.

In this necklace, small Styrofoam balls are used as bases; experiment with different shapes and sizes of foam to sculpt your own funky beads. In this project, time is needed to roll out the clay into a thin sheet and wrap it around the Styrofoam cores. Apoxie Sculpt was used in this project because it has a medium-long working time. Other clays can be used as well, but we don't recommend any quick-setting clays because you may not have time to form and refine your beads.

Oversize-Bead Necklace
Designed by Rachel Haab

WHAT YOU'LL NEED

- Gloves
- Apoxie Sculpt (Aves)
- Olive oil
- Plastic clay roller
- Teflon sheet
- Small Styrofoam balls, from ½ to 2 inches (13mm to 5cm) in diameter
- Craft knife
- Heavy-gauge wire
- Rubber-tipped clay tool
- Bowl or baking dish
- Two crimp beads
- Heavy nylon-coated wire or cable, long enough to make necklace plus a few extra inches on each end
- Flat-nose or crimping pliers
- Scissors
- ¾ yard (68.5cm) ribbon about ½ to ¾ inch (13mm to 2cm) wide
- Sewing needle and thread to match the ribbon

1

2

3

4

5

6

1. Wearing gloves, knead together the two-part clay until the clay is a uniform color. Using an oiled clay roller, roll out a very thin sheet of clay (about ¹⁄₁₆ inch [1.5mm]) onto the Teflon.

2. Brush away any excess debris from the Styrofoam balls. Place one ball on the sheet of clay and begin wrapping the clay around it, pinching the clay together and pressing it to the ball as you go.

3. When the ball is covered, tear away any excess clay. Pinch together any open seams of clay and begin to even out the surface by pressing on the bead with your fingers.

4. Roll the ball between the palms of your hands to create a smooth, even surface.

5. If you find any air bubbles as you roll the ball, use a craft knife to cut open the clay and let the air escape. Press the cut clay back together and reroll the ball.

6. When the bead is smooth, pierce the bead with the heavy-gauge wire to create a hole. Small pieces of Styrofoam may be pushed out of the other end as the wire runs through the bead—just brush away any excess foam.

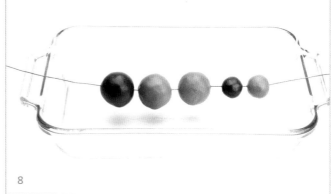

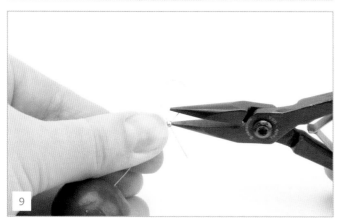

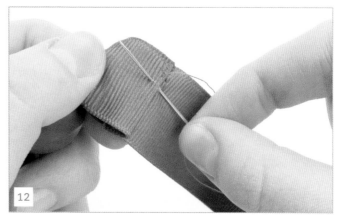

7. Piercing the bead with the wire may have created a rough edge around the hole. Smooth this by pressing the clay back onto the bead using a clay shaper.

8. Repeat steps 1–7 to create more beads in different shades of clay and different sizes. Let the beads cure by laying the wire across a baking dish or bowl to suspend the beads as they cure.

9. For the necklace closure, thread a crimp bead onto the nylon-coated wire or cable. Bring the end of the coated wire back through the crimp bead and use crimping pliers or flat-nose pliers to flatten the crimp bead, leaving a medium-sized loop of cord free.

10. String all of the beads onto the coated wire. At the end of the wire, repeat step 9 to add a loop at the other end of the necklace. Clip away any excess wire. Cut two 12-inch (30.5cm) lengths of ribbon.

11. Thread one piece of ribbon through one of the nylon-coated loops and fold the raw edge under twice to create a clean edge.

12. Use a needle and thread to stitch down the folded ribbon and secure it to the loop. Tie a knot and cut away excess thread. Repeat steps 11–12 on the other end of the necklace. Close the necklace by tying a bow with the two ribbons.

Sculpting over an Existing Form

If you enjoy sculpting, there are many design possibilities with this project. A mushroom is a kitschy retro design that's easy to sculpt, and it makes a unique housing for the mini kaleidoscope hidden inside. Clay can be added in stages, allowing for intricate details. Magic-Sculpt Clay gives you a long working time, is very durable when cured, and can be painted with your favorite colors after curing. Magic-Sculpt smoothes with water, which helps the artist easily refine a large sculpted piece such as these mushrooms. This clay also has a somewhat porous surface when dry which absorbs and adheres to acrylic paint well. However, any clay with a medium to long curing time can be used to sculpt this project. The variations are endless, so these make great personalized gifts.

Mushroom Kaleidoscopes
Designed by Sherri Haab

WHAT YOU'LL NEED

- Mini Kaleidoscope Kit (Craft Supplies USA, item # 050-7040)
- Magic-Sculpt Clay (Magic-Sculpt)
- Needle tool
- 600-grit wet/dry sanding paper
- Several paintbrushes for applying gesso, paints, and varnish
- Gesso
- Acrylic paints
- Acrylic antiquing medium (Plaid)
- Soft cloth
- Water-based varnish

1. Build your kaleidoscope according to the manufacturer's instructions. This photo shows the parts and relative placement of the pieces. Keep the lens and parts clean as you put them together.
2. Sculpt the mushroom shape in two stages. Wearing gloves, mix enough clay and catalyst to make a ball of clay to form the stem portion of the mushroom that will cover the kaleidoscope. Knead the clay thoroughly and wrap around the sides of the kaleidoscope.
3. Shape the clay wider around the end or base of the stem.
4. Shape the clay around the kaleidoscope tube, being careful to avoid covering the end and viewing caps. Let this part begin to set up while you form the cap of the mushroom. It can be fully cured or partially set up when the cap portion is added.
5. Mix another ball of clay with catalyst to make the mushroom cap. Shape the clay into a domed shape that's flat on the bottom.
6. Use a needle tool to pierce a hole in the center of the cap shape for the viewing end. Make the hole the same size as the viewing cap.

7. Score lines around the hole on the underside of the domed cap with the needle tool.

8. Place the cap onto the top of the stem, carefully aligning the viewing hole.

9. Press and smooth the cap to make sure it's attached to the stem and reshape as needed.

10. Smooth the top of the cap, making sure the hole is intact.

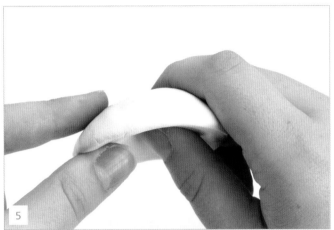

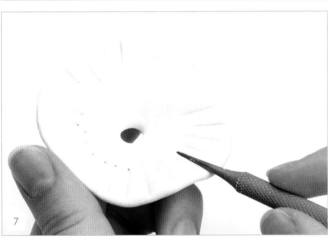

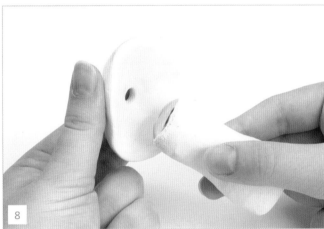

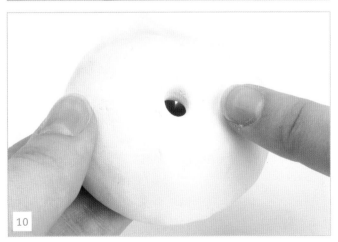

11

12

13

14

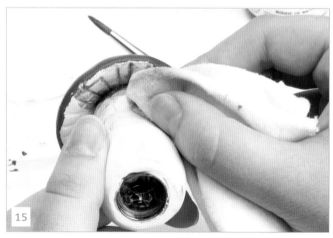

15

11. Let the mushroom set overnight until the clay is fully cured. Sand the outside with 600-grit wet/dry sandpaper to help the paint adhere.

12. Use a paintbrush to coat the surface with gesso, which is a primer for the paint. Let dry.

13. Paint the cap and stem as desired with acrylic paints. Let the layers dry before adding details such as polka dots. Let the paint dry thoroughly.

14. Stain the painted surface with an acrylic antiquing medium.

15. Use a damp cloth to wipe the stain off the surface, leaving paint in the recessed details. Seal the surface with water-based varnish if desired after the stain dries.

Repairing and Redesigning Vintage Jewelry

Beautiful antique jewelry is often found with broken or missing pieces, making it unwearable. Resin clay can be used to make replicas and repairs that are identical to the original piece. For example, in this project, a pair of floral earrings with broken petals was restored using resin clay. Resin clay is a wonderful medium for repairing jewelry because it can be made to look like almost any material. Recreate delicate parts of jewelry that have been broken away and adhere pieces back together using two-part clay. Magic-Sculpt, which we used here, is an easy to use clay with a medium curing time, giving the artist time to refine the details of this vintage piece. Also, the white clay is a great blank canvas for adding color to match an existing piece. Any two-part clay can be used for this project. After repairing a piece or two, you'll find yourself raiding the antique shop for the broken jewelry everyone has left behind.

Vintage Jewelry Repair and Redesign
by Michelle Haab

WHAT YOU'LL NEED

- Gloves
- Magic-Sculpt Clay (Magic-Sculpt)
- Broken or damaged antique or vintage jewelry
- Needle tool
- Clay shaper
- Metal bracelet blank (Gilding the Lily)
- Pearls or beads for embellishing the flowers
- Head pins
- Wire cutters
- Metal flowers for embellishment
- Paintbrush for finishing
- Gloss sealer or FolkArt Acrylic Antiquing Medium (Plaid) (optional)

1. Wearing gloves, knead appropriate amounts of color until the clay resembles the jewelry color. Read about different coloring techniques on page 26 to find the best match for your piece. After the desired color is achieved, mix the colored clay with an equal amount of the catalyst.
2. Using your fingers, flatten a small piece of clay and pinch one side to resemble a petal.
3. Use a needle tool to score the center and add texture to the surface.
4. Fasten the new clay piece to the jewelry, pressing it in place.
5. Use a clay shaper or needle tool to smooth small amounts of leftover clay between the two pieces. Let cure. Repeat steps 2–5 to finish the rest of your flowers. Let cure.
6. Add pearls to metal flower blanks by threading them onto a head pin and pulling through the center of the flower.
7. Make a 90-degree angle with the head pin at the base of the flower and use pliers to make several bends in the head pin.

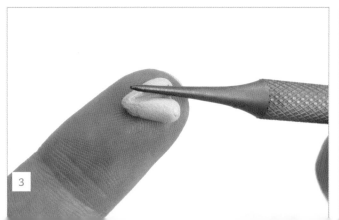

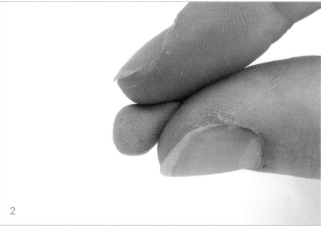

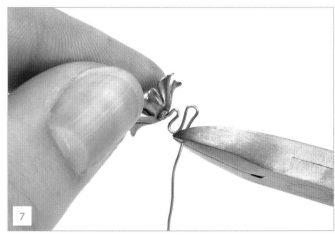

This will help the flower hold more securely to the bracelet when it is added. Remove any excess wire. Set aside.

8. To add the flowers to a metal bracelet blank, knead together more two-part clay, this time in the color you would like the bracelet to be covered with. Mix thoroughly until uniform color is achieved. Press small amounts of clay onto the metal bracelet blank on both sides and smooth with your fingers until the clay is flush with the edges of the bracelet.

9. Press the metal flowers and the antique pieces into the clay on the blank while keeping the back in place and pressing firmly against it. Let cure. When the clay is hard after a few hours, add more clay underneath the antique flower if needed to secure the piece to the bracelet blank.

10. After allowing the piece to set for 4 hours, use a paintbrush to add a gloss finish or stain, depending on the original look of the jewelry.

Creating a Hollow Form

Small objects and ephemera fill this antique-style heart box pendant. Although it's made using resin clay and plastic, this piece has a vintage feel to it and can be stained with paint to look like wood or porcelain framing glass. Because Apoxie Sculpt is somewhat soft, it is great for smoothing and blending edges such as the seams around the walls of the heart box, but any two-part clay can be used for this project. The small viewing window on this piece was recycled from old packaging; this transparent, thin plastic is usually used in gift boxes or to package tech items and toys. A small piece of clear, thin plastic such as acrylic can also be used. Fill your box with special trinkets, scraps of paper, buttons, branches, or other found objects.

Hollow Pendant

Designed by Rachel Haab

WHAT YOU'LL NEED

- Paper
- Pencil
- Scissors
- Small heart-shaped Klay Kutter (Kemper Tools) or cookie cutter
- Gloves
- Apoxie Sculpt (Aves)
- Plastic clay roller
- Olive oil
- Shade-Tex Rubbing Plate (Scratch Art)
- Pearl Ex Powdered Pigments, Pearl White (Jacquard Products)
- Craft knife
- Patterned piece of silverware
- Clear acetate plastic or acrylic sheet (recycled from old packaging)
- Pen
- Rubber stamp (optional)
- Small objects for filling the pendant
- 6 inches (15cm) of 22- to 24-gauge wire
- Round-nose pliers
- Wire cutters
- Acrylic antiquing medium (Plaid)
- Cloth
- White acrylic paint
- Necklace chain

1. Trace the desired shape of your pendant onto a piece of paper using a pencil. It's helpful to place the heart-shaped cutter in the middle of the shape to make sure there will be enough space around the plastic window. Cut out the paper pattern. This template will be your size guide throughout the project.

2. Wearing gloves, knead together the two-part clay until the clay is a uniform color. Roll out a sheet of clay using an oiled clay roller. This sheet of clay is about ⅛ inch (3mm) thick.

3. The back of the window box is created first. Press a Shade-Tex Rubbing Plate into the clay to create texture. Remove the rubbing plate, and using your finger, lightly brush Pearl Ex powder into the surface of the clay to highlight the texture.

4. Place the size-guide paper onto the clay and use it as a pattern to cut out your shape. Remove excess clay and set this piece aside.

5. Roll out a rope of clay about ⅛ inch (3mm) thick and long enough to wrap around the entire box. Use an old piece of silverware for texture. This will be the wall around your window box. Cut away excess clay using a craft knife, leaving a thin strip of clay.

6. Press the strip of clay up around the perimeter of the back piece, leaving the top of the box open, and cut away any excess clay with the craft knife. Use your finger to gently blend the seam where the base of the box and the wall meet. Place the size-guide pattern on top of the wall to make sure the wall stays straight and perpendicular to the base. Adjust the wall if needed. Let cure for a few hours or until it holds its shape.

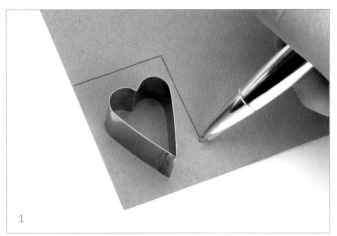

1

2

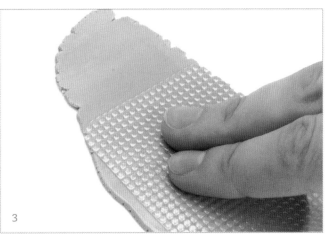

3

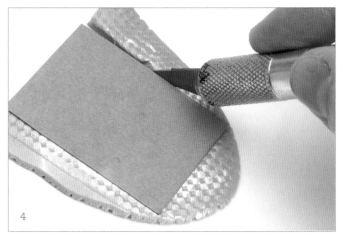

4

7. Trace around the paper pattern onto the plastic using a pen. Cut away about ⅛ inch (3mm) inside the lines of the rectangle in order to create a piece of plastic that's slightly smaller than the pattern. Set aside.

8. Wearing gloves, knead together the two-part clay until the clay is a uniform color. Roll out a thin sheet of clay using a clay roller. Cut two rectangles out of the clay using the paper pattern as a guide. Use a texture plate or rubber stamp to texture one of the rectangles. Use the heart cutter to cut hearts out of both pieces. Remove the excess clay.

9. Place the plastic rectangle on top of the untextured piece, then place the textured piece on top of the plastic, sandwiching the plastic between the two heart cutouts. Around the edge, blend the two sheets of clay together, hiding any edges of the acrylic.

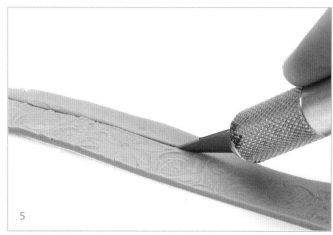

5

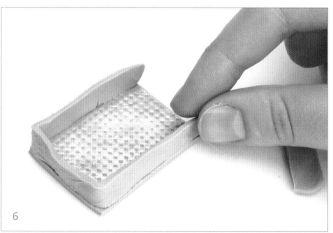

6

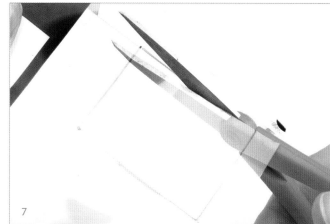

7

8

9

10. Press the front piece onto the top of the box and blend the seams around the edge. Let cure.

11. Place the small objects into the box.

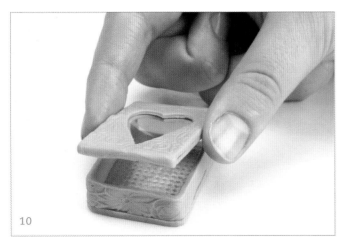

10

12. Bend a 3-inch (7.5cm) piece of wire over round-nose pliers to create a soft turn in the wire.

13. Twist the two ends of wire together several times to close the loop. Clip away any excess wire. Repeat steps 12 and 13 to make another hook. Set aside.

14. Wearing gloves, knead together a small portion of the two-part clay until the clay is a uniform color. This will be the lid of your box. Mold a thick rectangle and press it into the top of the box. Use your fingers to refine the edges of the lid after you press it in. Use the silverware to texture the top of the box as in step 5.

15. Press the wire hooks made in steps 12 and 13 into the top of the box. Let cure.

16. Avoiding the clear window, rub antiquing medium onto the surface of the box to accentuate the texture.

11

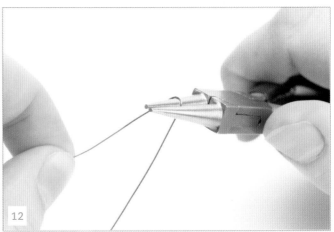

12

13

14

17. Rub away excess paint with a slightly damp cloth. Let dry. Repeat step 16 using white paint to highlight the piece and wipe away any excess paint. Let dry. Finish by connecting to a necklace chain.

15

16

17

Designing Realistic Flowers and Leaves

Lumina clay is ideal for this project. It's very strong and flexible, even in thin layers, and has a slightly translucent quality that resembles porcelain. For this reason, vibrant and realistic flowers can be made with delicate petals and thin details without being too fragile for everyday wear. Lumina can also be used for many other designs where a very thin piece of clay is needed. The petals in this project are roughly torn from a ball of clay to create a somewhat rugged, organic-looking edge. However, these petals can be sculpted freehand or cut out of a sheet of clay using a craft knife or clay cutter if desired. Find inspiration from all different kinds of flowers to create your own bouquet of jewelry!

Pink Flower Necklace
Designed by Rachel Haab

WHAT YOU'LL NEED

- Lumina clay (Activa Products)
- Toothpicks
- Oil paint in desired colors in yellow and pink or red
- Craft knife
- Needle tool
- Paintbrush for applying stain
- Acrylic antiquing medium
- Cloth
- Waxed paper
- Two-part epoxy adhesive (quick-setting)
- Metal Filigree Circle (Vintaj)
- Jump rings or wire
- Necklace or chain

1. Pinch off a small amount of Lumina clay and add a tiny amount of yellow oil paint for color. Knead in the color. Roll out a small ball of the clay into a small cylinder. This will be the center of the flower. Set aside.

2. Divide the Lumina clay into three medium-sized balls. Use a toothpick to add varying amounts of oil paint to each ball. This will create the three shades of petals for the flower. Mix the paint into each clay ball thoroughly.

3. Begin with the darkest shade of clay. Use your fingers to pinch away a thin petal shape from the ball of clay. Slightly smooth the rugged edge of the petal using your finger.

4. Press this petal against the center cylinder to begin the flower.

5. Continue adding petals to the flower until you reach the desired size. On this flower, we began with the darkest colored petals in the center and gradually added the lighter shades of petals to the exterior.

6. Use a craft knife to cut off the excess clay on the back of the flower center so that it lays flat.

7. Mix up another small ball of Lumina and add yellow oil paint for color. Press it into the center of the flower.

8. Use a needle tool to stipple the surface of the clay center.

9. When the flower has dried, use a paintbrush to stain the flower center with acrylic antiquing medium.

10. After painting the flower, wipe any excess paint away with a damp cloth. Let dry.

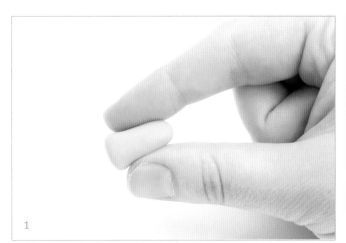

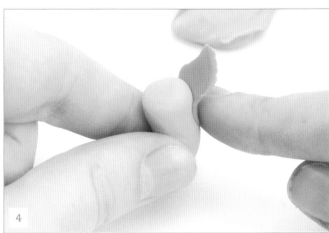

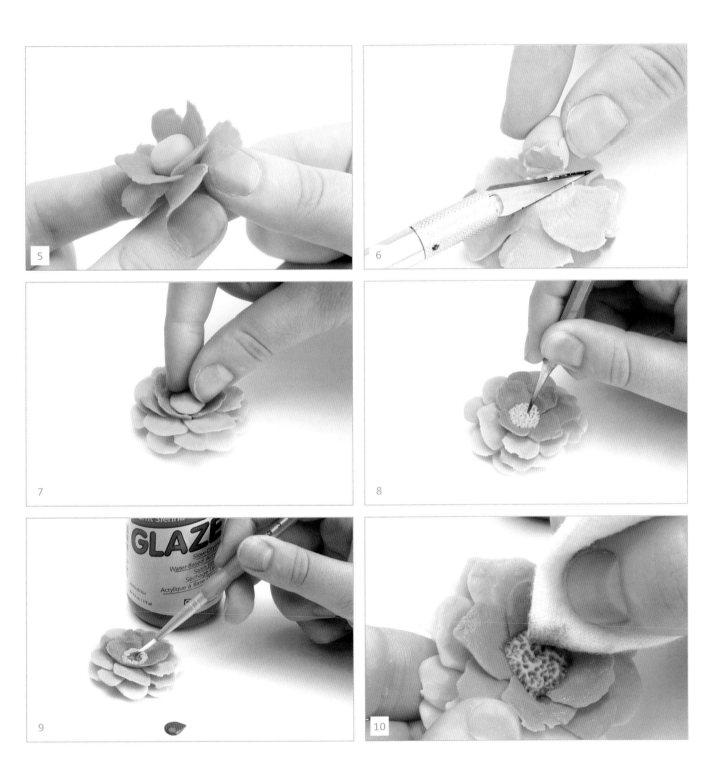

11. On a sheet of waxed paper, mix some quick-setting epoxy adhesive according to the instructions on the package. Use a toothpick to drop epoxy onto the flat back of the flower.

12. Press the metal filigree into the epoxy glue and hold in place until the glue has dried. Make sure the filigree overlaps the edge of the base jut a bit so there is a border of metal loops free. These loops will provide areas to attach a necklace by jump ring or wire later. Let dry.

13. Use wire-wrapping techniques shown on page 37 or jump rings to attach the flower to a necklace or chain. This photo shows the connection of jump rings and chain to the filigree backing of the flower.

Creating Chain Links

Give a delicate look to this funky bold chain by adding light flakes of gold leaf and a single gold-coated link. The necklace's industrial style gives it the illusion of heaviness and weight even though the resulting piece is light and wearable. The great thing about using quick-setting clay, like the KlayResin used for this project, is that you can create chain links one at a time and let them quickly cure while you add a new one. This way, the links won't stick together. Personalize your look by playing around with the shapes of the links—you can create any geometric shape and nontraditional organic-looking chain.

Steel Chain Necklace

Designed by Michelle Haab

WHAT YOU'LL NEED

- KlayResin in Urban Steel (Sherri Haab Designs)
- Craft knife
- Gloves
- Water
- Gold leaf
- Soft paintbrush
- Chain-nose pliers
- Length of chain
- Two jump rings
- Clasp
- Thin strip of leather
- Teflon working surface
- Water-based clear varnish

1. Slice off one medium-sized section of clay (at least 1 inch [2.5cm] long) at a time to make one link. In this project, clay is mixed as needed for each link. Knead the clay quickly until uniform in color.

2. Roll a clay rope on a Teflon surface until the desired thickness (at least ⅝ inch [1.5cm]) is reached.

3. Make the first link on a flat surface by forming the clay rope roughly into the desired shape and overlapping the ends to join the link.

4. Blend the joint using your fingers. A little bit of water can also be used to blend the seam and create a smooth finish.

5. As the resin clay is curing, it may be necessary to reshape the link. Use your fingers to shape and smooth the piece. Let cure.

1

2

3

6. Continue the chain by repeating the steps, remembering to thread the next clay rope through the previous link before joining the ends. As each new link cures, leave enough space between them to make sure it doesn't stick to the link it's being joined to.

7. When the clay has set but still has a slightly tacky surface, add small flakes of gold leaf. This is best done by using a paintbrush to lift and apply flakes of gold leaf to the piece, then using your dry fingers to press and smooth the leaf onto the link.

8. To add a solid-gold link to the chain, wrap larger pieces of full gold-leaf sheets around a link while the clay is still curing.

9. Use a soft paintbrush to remove any excess gold leaf from the link. Add this link into the chain and allow the piece to cure fully. Brush on a layer of clear varnish to protect the gold leaf.

10. Add a metal chain to the clay links by using chain-nose pliers to open a link at the end of the chain. Thread it onto the clay chain and then close the metal link with pliers to secure. Repeat on the other end of the chain.

11. Thread a strip of leather through the last clay link. Pull the leather through until the chain link is in the center of the length of cord.

12. Begin weaving the leather cord through the metal chain. Do this by pushing one end of the leather cord down through the metal link and the other end up through the metal link and continue alternating until you reach the end of the chain. Tie off the ends of leather using a square knot for security. Trim away any excess cord.

GALLERY: MOLDING AND SCULPTING TECHNIQUES

1. **Blue Bird with Heart** by Leslie Blackford. Makin's clay sculpted over armature, wire, and acrylic paint. *Photo by the artist.*

2. **Flowers** by Yukiko Miyai. ClayCraft by DECO. *Photo by Tim Jones.*

3. **Garden Ghost** by Denise Baldwin. Aves Apoxie Clay over recycled light bulb, acrylic paints, and matte spray finish. *Photo by the artist.*

Contributing Artists

Denise Baldwin
oddimagination.etsy.com

Leslie Blackford
www.moodywoods.com

Melanie Brooks
www.earthenwoodstudio.com

Robert Dancik
www. fauxbone.wordpress.com

Yukiko Miyai
decoclay.typepad.com

Cassy Muronaka
www.cassymuronaka.com

Alita Porter
www.doricdragons.co.uk

Osamu Watanabe
osamuwatanabe.web.fc2.com

Resources

Activa Products
activaproducts.com
Lumina Clay

Aves
avesstudio.com
Apoxie Clay, Apoxie Sculpt, Aves Safety
Solvent

Craft Supplies USA
woodturnerscatalog.com
Mini Kaleidoscope Kit, item # 050-7040

DECO CLAY
decoclay.com
ClayCraft

Gilding the Lily
gildingthelilyvintage.blogspot.com
Metal bracelet blanks

**Jacquard Products/Rupert Gibbon
and Spider Inc.**
jacquardproducts.com
Pearl Ex Powdered Pigments

Kemper Tools
kempertools.com
Klay Kutters and clay-working tools

Makin's Clay
makinsclay.com
Makin's Clay

Magic-Sculpt
magic-sculpt.com
Magic-Sculpt Epoxy Clay

Metal Clay Supply
metalclaysupply.com
MultiMandrel

Milliput Company
milliput.com
Milliput Epoxy Putty

Nunn Design
nunndesign.com
Bezels

Objects and Elements
objectsandelements.com
Staple bezels and findings

Plaid
plaidonline.com
Mod Podge, acrylic paint, and acrylic
mediums

Robert's Real Faux Bone
fauxbone.com
Faux Bone, sanding tools and materials

Scratch Art
scratchart.com
Shade-Tex Rubbing Plates

Sherri Haab Designs
sherrihaab-shop.com
KlayResin, metal ring blanks

Tandy Leather Factory
tandyleatherfactory.com
Leather stamps

Vintaj Natural Brass Co.
vintaj.com
Metal findings

Project Index

Scrimshaw Pendant
Page 40

Raku Beads Bracelet
Page 45

Coral Branch Pendant
Page 48

Copper Cuff Bracelet
Page 52

Clover Charm Pendant
Page 60

Filigree Button Ring
Page 64

Stained Glass Earrings
Page 69

Geode Ring
Page 73

Bead Mosaic Pendant
Page 80

Graffiti Bracelet
Page 84

Resin Clay Inlay Pendant
Page 88

Desserts and Pastry
Treats, *Page 92*

Wax Seal Ring
Page 104

Red Rose Pendant
Page 108

Oversize-Bead Necklace
Page 112

Mushroom Kaleidoscopes
Page 116

Vintage Jewelry Repair
and Redesign, *Page 121*

Hollow Pendant
Page 124

Pink Flower Necklace
Page 130

Steel Chain Necklace
Page 135

Index